HEBREWS

The Pre-eminence of Christ.

By Jack Sequeira

JACK SEQUEIRA MINISTRIES

Hebrews: The Pre-eminence of Christ
Jack Sequeira

Edited by Edwin A. Schwisow
Cover and Layout by Ron Burgard, Macmouser Graphics

Published by Jack Sequeira Ministries
PMB #244, 3760 Market Street NE
Salem, OR 97301
www.jacksequeira.org

Unless otherwise indicated, Scripture is taken from the *New Iinternational Version (NIV).*

Printed in the United States of America

ISBN: 0-9826404-1-8

Second Printing, 2011

Table of Contents

Preface 5

1   Christ—God's Final Word *(Hebrews 1:1-3)* 7

2   Christ—Greater than the Angels *(Hebrews 1:4-2:4)* 14

3   Christ—God Who Exalted Man *(Hebrews 2:5-13)* 22

4   God Suffers for Man *(Hebrews 2:14-18)* 29

5   Christ—Greater than Moses *(Hebrews 3:1-6)* 36

6   Warnings from Israel's History *(Hebrews 3:7-19)* 44

7   Christ—The True Sabbath Rest *(Hebrews 4:1-13)* 51

8   Christ—Our High Priest *(Hebrews 4:14-5:10)* 59

9   The Cost of Abandoning Christ *(Hebrews 5:11—6:1-12)* 67

10 The Certainty of God's Promises *(Hebrews 6:13-20)* 75

11 Preeminence of Christ's Priesthood *(Hebrews 7:1-28)* 82

12 Christ—Priest of a Better Covenant *(Hebrews 8:1-13)* 90

13 The Heavenly Sanctuary *(Hebrews 9:1-28)* 98

14 Christ's Perfect Sacrifice *(Hebrews 10:1-22)* 106

15 The Cost of Unbelief *(Hebrews 10:23-39)* 114

16 Hall of Faith *(Hebrews 11:1-40)* 122

17 Christ—The Supreme Example *(Hebrews 12:1-4)* 130

18 God's Refining Process *(Hebrews 12:5-11)* 138

19 Living Under the New Covenant *(Hebrews 12:12-29)* 145

20 Living the Christian Life *(Hebrews 13:1-25)* 153

Dedication

This book
is lovingly dedicated
to the Mooncotch family
in appreciation for their
many years support
of Jack Sequeira Ministries.

Preface

The author of Hebrews addresses the Epistle to the Hebrews to Jewish Christians in New Testament times—believers pressured and persecuted to put aside the simplicity of faith-based Christianity and return to the ritual requirements of Judaism.

This epistle was also written, I believe, to help prepare these believers for the shocking destruction of the Jerusalem temple in 70 A.D. As long as the temple stood, God was seen as present among His people. The destruction of the temple would mean that the glory of the Lord had left His people (1 Samuel 4:21)—except as the Christians held tenaciously to their faith in Jesus, the true Glory of Israel.

The writer of Hebrews affirms that Jesus Christ answers every human need, for all time. No other book in Scripture presents more fully the doctrine of Christology, with Jesus Christ as the center of faith, presented as unshakeable reality for all believers to the end of time.

The book of Hebrews alternates between encouragement and warning. Since the Jewish believers were familiar with the Old Testament, the writer of Hebrews clearly demonstrates that all the types and shadows of the Old Testament were fulfilled in the holy history of Jesus Christ, their Messiah (Luke 24:25-27). Hence, the key word in these passages is the word "better." Christ is a better revelation, a better Moses, a better hope and rest, a better sacrifice, a better possession, and a better priest. The warnings in Hebrews make it clear that to give up faith in Christ, the Source of salvation, is to give up hope of salvation altogether. It is a matter of life and death.

Problems faced by 21st century Christians, while not identical to those in the 1st century, are amazingly similar. Since September 11, 2001 ("911"), terrorism has become a much more visible threat, even as prophecy affirms that these are the last days of world history. Prophets Daniel and Jeremiah both make it clear that just before the Second Advent of Christ, a generation of Christians will face a time of trouble of unparalleled intensity (see Daniel 12:1 and Jeremiah 30:7).

What will make this time of trouble so terrible? The Old Testament gospel prophet, Isaiah, spells it out clearly in Isaiah 54:5-8. The last generation of Christians will experience God-abandonment, similar, but to a lesser degree, to that which Jesus faced on the cross when He cried out, "My God, my God, why have You forsaken me?" (Matthew 27:46).

The final battle in the great controversy between Christ, the Savior of the world, and Satan, the enemy of souls, is the Battle of Armageddon, described in Revelation 16:12-16. This is not a political war, as some believe, but a spiritual conflict. The issue at that time will be, Can the gospel produce a people with the faith of Jesus (not just faith in Jesus), as He demonstrated it on the cross?

Through their unshakeable faith, these Christians will fully demonstrate the power of the gospel to save mankind from the principle of self (the law of sin), confirmed by Revelation 7:13 and 14. This, in turn, will light the earth with the glory of Jesus Christ.

These expository studies of the Epistle of Hebrews will help establish God's people in Christ, that their faith may be unmovable even amid great tribulation. Jesus makes it clear indeed that "you shall know the truth, and the truth shall make you free" (John 8:32, 36).

Jack Sequeira Ministries
PMB #244
3760 Market Street NE
Salem, OR 97301

www.jacksequeira.org

CHAPTER 1
Christ—God's Final Word
Hebrews 1:1-3

Our world is becoming unglued, and every attempt to solve its problems are failing. The future looks bleak. What the Bible predicted about the last days is coming true. Men and women everywhere are asking in desperation, "Is there no hope?"

The answer to this most important question is, "Yes! Jesus Christ is the answer to every human need!"

Of all the books in the New Testament—in fact, of all the books in the Bible—the Epistle to the Hebrews is the clearest and most systematic presentation of Christ as the Savior of the world. Hebrews clearly explains who Christ is and what His earthly mission was, as He redeemed mankind and reconciled our race to a holy God. But more than this, it presents Christ as a great, sympathetic, and merciful High Priest in the heavenly sanctuary, interceding on behalf of those who believe in Him.

In our study of this epistle, we will carefully examine Hebrews' message and significance. Hebrews was originally written to Jewish Christians of New Testament times who, because of severe persecution from Jews who had not accepted Christ, were in constant danger of giving up their faith and turning back to Judaism. This is why Hebrews points to Christ as the reality—the fulfillment—of everything God promised the Jews in the Old Testament through types and shadows. Christ is God's only solution for mankind's sin problem. To reject Him, says Hebrews' author, is to incur eternal damnation.

As we study through the book of Hebrews, we will discover a key word—"*better*". Hebrews 1 and 2 present Christ as the "better" revelation; Chapter 3 presents Christ as "better" than Moses, the great deliverer of the Jewish nation from Egyptian bondage. Chapter 4 presents Christ as a "better" rest. Chapters 5 to 7 present Christ as a "better" hope and "better" priesthood. Chapter 9 presents Him as a "better" sacrifice and Chapter 10 as a "better" possession. Finally, Chapter 11 portrays Christ as a "better" resurrection.

The writer of Hebrews concludes with chapters 12 and 13, exhorting his readers not to give up their faith in Christ, no matter what happens to them.

Who Wrote Hebrews?

In this chapter we focus on Hebrews 1, primarily its introduction in verses 1-3. But before we do that, we need to deal with a question on the minds of many Bible students: Who wrote Hebrews?

Some King James Version editions of the Bible present Paul as the author of Hebrews. Headings vary, but a typical one reads, "The Epistle of Paul to the Hebrews."

Yet, at the very end of the epistle, these very same editions note, "Written to the Hebrews from Italy by Timothy."

Who *really* is the author? Bible students still discuss this question, for in actual fact the author is unknown. True, many believe it to be Paul. Hebrews' theology definitely sounds like Paul's, but its Greek language style is by no means Pauline. So many believe that one of Paul's students wrote Hebrews—perhaps Timothy, Barnabas, Luke, Silas, or Apollos.

I personally take the position that Paul wrote Hebrews—but not originally in Greek. He wrote it instead in Aramaic, the common language of the Jews of his time, and the epistle was then translated by someone else from the Aramaic into the Greek. Since we no longer have the original manuscripts of this or any book of the Bible, we can never be absolutely sure, but evidence for this hypothesis is strong.

Not once does Paul mention his name in the introduction to Hebrews, as he normally does in his epistles. He omits his own name, I believe, because he well knows that many Jews consider him an arch traitor.

In Acts 21, Luke tells of Paul returning to Jerusalem from his third journey to Asia Minor and of his being told by James to follow the ceremony of cleansing so that the Jews will realize that he is *not* against them. This cleansing process takes seven days.

Even so, Acts 21:27 and 28 tells us, "When the seven days were nearly over, some Jews from the province of Asia saw Paul at the temple. They stirred up the whole crowd and seized him, shouting, 'Men of Israel, help us! This is the man who teaches all men everywhere against our people (*that is, the Jews*) and our law and this place (*that is, the temple*). And besides, he has brought Greeks (*that is, Gentiles*) into the temple area and defiled the holy place.'"

Paul is arrested, imprisoned, and eventually transported in chains to Rome, where he ministers for a time and finally is martyred.

At the time Hebrews was written, many Jews were prejudiced against Paul and, knowing this, he chooses not to mention himself as author of the book. This is my personal view.

But whatever position we take, one thing is absolutely clear. The Epistle to the Hebrews is an inspired document, belonging part and parcel to the Word of God.

The Introduction

Having laid this foundation, we look briefly at the epistle's introduction, where Christ is presented as God's final Word to mankind. In the Old Testament, God spoke through prophets, but their message was incomplete in that they used types and shadows to point to the better things to come in Christ. But when Christ Himself came to this world, salvation became a reality. Christ, then, is the final Word of God to mankind—the reality of the plan of salvation promised to the human race through types and shadows in the Old Testament.

We begin by reading Hebrews 1:1-3. "In the past God spoke to our forefathers through the prophets at many times and in various ways, but in these last days he has spoken to us by his Son, whom he appointed heir of all things, and through whom he made the universe. The Son is the radiance of God's glory and exact representation of his being, sustaining all things by his powerful word. After he had provided purification for sins, he sat down on the right hand of the Majesty in heaven."

For almost 4,000 years God had been promising sinful man a Savior. After sin entered in the Garden of Eden, He told Adam and Eve a Savior would come, as He later told Moses. But in a special way He promised a Savior to the Jewish nation through Abraham and gave the Jews many symbols, types, and shadows to remind them of this wonderful promise. In Paul's introduction of the Epistle to the Romans, he tells of God's dealing with the Jewish nation.

In Romans 1 and 2 Paul paints a dark and dismal picture of mankind—focusing first on the Gentiles and then on his own people, the Jews, and concluding that all are equally lost without Christ.

Paul realizes, of course, that his Jewish readers will immediately bristle and say that such a position denies any advantage to the devout, practicing Jew.

So in Romans 3, verses 1 and 2, Paul answers that objection and explains that there is indeed an advantage for the Jews: "What advantage, then, is there in being a Jew, or what value is there in circumcision? Much in every way! First of all, they have been entrusted with the very words of God."

God gave His laws to the Gentiles through their consciences and through nature. But to the Jews He gave an explicit knowledge of Himself through the written Word. Therefore the Jews had the advantage of the law and all the types and symbols that pointed to Christ.

Symbols Fulfilled

Those types and shadows became reality about 2,000 years ago, when God kept His promise and sent His Son as this world's Redeemer. This is what the angel announced to the frightened shepherds. The story of Christ's birth is found in Luke 2:10: "But the angel said unto them (*the frightened shepherds*), 'Do not be afraid. I bring you good news of great joy that will be for all people.'"

This First Coming of Christ as the suffering servant to redeem fallen humanity unfortunately was greatly misunderstood, for the Jewish nation had been focusing primarily on the segments of Messianic prophecies that dealt with Christ's coming as a king and conqueror.

At the time Christ came, the Jews were under Roman bondage, and their greatest desire was to be liberated and restored as a great world power.

So the Jews had been selective in their reading of the prophecies about the First, Second, and Third Comings of Christ, emphasizing the wording that foretold His might and dominion.

Christ's Three Comings

The Old Testament Messianic prophecies present composite pictures of Messiah's ministry, without including time frames for each phase of His work.

A good example is found in Isaiah, the gospel prophet of the Old Testament. We find in Isaiah 11:1-9 that all three comings of Christ—all three phases of the plan of redemption—are combined, as if they were one event: "A shoot will come up from the stump of Jesse; from his roots a Branch will bear fruit. The Spirit of the Lord will rest on Him—the

Spirit of wisdom and of understanding, the Spirit of counsel and of power, the Spirit of knowledge and of the fear of the Lord—and he will delight in the fear of the Lord."

This first portion of the passage clearly deals with the First Coming of Christ. Jesus once stood up in the synagogue in his home town of Nazareth and declared, "The Spirit of the Lord is upon Me." Clearly this portion of the passage was fulfilled in the First Coming of Christ.

In the second half of verse 3 and through verse 4, however, we see a different picture: "He will not judge by what he sees with his eyes, or decide by what he hears with his ears; but with righteousness he will judge the needy, with justice he will give decisions for the poor of the earth. He shall strike the earth with a rod of his mouth; with the breath of his lips he will slay the wicked. Righteousness shall be his belt and faithfulness the sash around his waist."

Clearly this portion of the prophecy pertains to His Second Coming, when He will judge the world in righteousness.

Reading on in Isaiah 11:6-9, however, the prophet clearly describes the earth made new, which according to Revelation 21 and 22 will arrive on the scene at the Third Coming of Christ: "The wolf will live with the lamb, the leopard will lie down with the goat, the calf and the lion and the yearling together; and a little child will lead them. The cow will feed with the bear, their young will lie down together, and the lion shall eat straw like the ox. The infant will play near the hole of the cobra, and the young child put his hand into the viper's nest. They will neither harm nor destroy on all my holy mountain, for the earth will be full of the knowledge of the Lord as the waters cover the sea."

The First, Second, and Third Comings of Christ are combined together in this passage. This is true throughout the Old Testament. God did this, I believe, because humans are impatient and cannot stand delays. Between each of these comings of Christ, we now realize, come (in human terms) huge gaps of time. But as Jesus pointed out to His disciples, human beings are not able to handle such extended projections of time—Jesus said that there were many things He wanted to tell us that we are not able to bear. While time is immaterial to God because He lives in eternity, we humans are victims of time. We want everything now.

That is perhaps why plastic credit cards were invented—so we could buy everything and pay later, enjoying things when we want them. Out of consideration for our limitations, God in His love and understanding—and because He knew we could not handle delays—placed these promises together as if they were one event.

We find the same thing in the New Testament. In Jesus' Matthew 24 prophecy about the destruction of Jerusalem and His Second Coming, He says nothing about a lapse of time between the first event (which was fulfilled in 70 A.D.) and His Second Coming, which is still future. It has been almost 2,000 years since the destruction of Jerusalem.

In the Epistle to the Hebrews, however, we find the whole plan of salvation laid out, including the purposes of Christ's first, second, and third returns to earth.

The study of that plan, therefore, was not only important to Jewish Christians in Paul's day who were in danger of reverting to Judaism. It is relevant today to those who await Jesus' Second Coming. We are living in an era when men's hearts are failing because there seems little hope for the future. Every solution of man is failing. Legislation has tried and failed. Giving freedom from all external moral codes has been attempted, only to create greater problems in society. Now many favor harsher police enforcement and stiffer punishment, but even these are not producing the desired results. Every human solution to the sin problem has failed in the past and is failing today.

Desperately, some nations reached out to exotic theories of government, including Marxism, hoping thereby to solve the sin problem. Karl Marx promised, after all, that his ideology—a philosophy he called dialectical materialism—could redeem man from exploitation and eradicate its greedy behavior. Yet, countries that have tried Marxism have failed utterly to eradicate selfishness.

There is no human solution to the sin problem—physical, material, or economic. There is only one solution, only one hope, and that is in Jesus Christ.

As we examine the message of the Epistle to the Hebrews, it is my sincere prayer that our faith will grow so strong, unshakeable, and fully established in Christ that nothing can affect it. And when that great time of trouble predicted in Scripture strikes, may we be able to say with the Apostle Paul, "I know in whom I have believed and that He is able to save me to the uttermost" (Hebrews 7:25) when Christ comes in the clouds of heaven.

This wonderful Epistle to the Hebrews was preserved as part of the Bible to establish Christian believers in Jesus Christ.

Summary

Let us read again the first three verses of Hebrews: "In the past God spoke to our forefathers through the prophets at many times and in various ways, but in these last days he has spoken to us by his Son, whom he appointed heir of all things, and through whom he made the universe. The Son is the radiance of God's glory and the exact representation of his being, sustaining all things by his powerful word."

Jesus Christ is not only our Creator, He is our Redeemer: "Who being the brightness of His glory and the express image of His person."

When Philip asks Jesus in John 14:8 and 9, "Lord, show us the Father," Jesus answers, "Have I been among you such a long time. . . anyone who has seen me has seen the Father."

In John 17:4 Jesus says to His Father, "I have brought you glory on the earth by completing the work you gave me to do." His work, of course, is to redeem the human race.

Jesus is the radiance of God's glory and the exact representation of His being, sustaining all things by His powerful Word. He spoke and it happened. He is the Word made flesh that dwelt among us and demonstrated to us His glory.

After He provided purification for sin and obtained salvation full and complete for all who accept that salvation, the book of Hebrews presents Jesus as sitting down at the right hand of the Majesty in heaven. Jesus does not go there to relax, but to intercede and defend those who have accepted Him as their Savior against the continual accusations of Satan.

May we, as we study this epistle, grow in grace and truth and in a knowledge of Jesus Christ until we are fully established in Him. Jesus said, "You shall know the truth, the truth about Him, and the truth will set you free" (John 8:32, 36).

CHAPTER 2
Christ—Greater than the Angels
Hebrews 1:4-2:4

In last chapter's introduction to the wonderful Epistle to the Hebrews, we looked at Hebrews 1:1-3, where Paul presents Christ as God's final Word to fallen humanity.

The Son of God assumed the form of unredeemed humanity and became the Son of Man, with a nature a little lower than the angels'.

Then, having fully redeemed mankind from its sin problem, He ascended into heaven and God exalted His name above every other name, including the angels'.

We read in Hebrews 2:9, for example: "But we see Jesus, who was made a little lower than the angels, now crowned with glory and honor because he suffered death, so that by the grace of God He might taste death for everyone."

In becoming a man Jesus lowered Himself and veiled His divinity in humanity. While on earth for 33 years, Jesus appeared to most to be just another human being, no different than His fellow Jews. Isaiah, the gospel prophet of the Old Testament, writes in Isaiah 53:2 that the Son of Man, like one of us, ". . . grew up before him like a tender shoot, and like a root out of dry ground. He had no beauty or majesty to attract us to him, nothing in his appearance that we should desire him. He was despised and rejected by men. . . " As a man, Christ looked no different than the rest of the human race He came to redeem.

The writer of Hebrews points out that Christ was originally greater than the angels. According to Psalm 8, angels are the highest form of created being. Only God is above them. Therefore, for Christ to be greater than the angels implies that He was not just a man, but a divine Being. The writer of Hebrews wants his readers to understand that Christ was no ordinary man. Some Jews who rejected Christ made the argument that He was just a carpenter's son—an ordinary human being. But no, He was more than a carpenter's son, says the writer of Hebrews. He was God manifested in the flesh to save the world.

At the beginning of his gospel, the Apostle John pens these memorable words about Jesus: "In the beginning was the Word, the Word was with God and the Word was God."

A few verses later, in John 1:14, we read: "The Word was made flesh and made his dwelling among us. We have seen his glory, the glory of the One and Only, who came from the Father, full of grace and truth."

The idea that Christ was not a mere man but God manifest in the flesh is clearly taught throughout the New Testament, and Paul presents the same idea in Philippians 2:6-11: "Who (*Christ*), being in very nature (*very substance*) God, did not consider equality with God something to be grasped." Theologians refer to this passage by a Greek term "*kenosis*", which means the self-emptying of Christ. It was not sin for Christ to equate Himself with God, for Jesus is divine. But He made Himself nothing (of no reputation, according to the King James Version). The Greek word means "emptied Himself". He deprived Himself of all His divine prerogatives and took the nature of a servant.

Christ was a unique human being, fully God and fully man, and this made Him special. In Hebrews 1 we find three reasons for Christ's superiority over the angels—reasons not only valid for the Jews of Paul's day but for us, today.

His Name Is Superior

In Hebrews 1:4 and 5 we read: "So, he (*Christ*) became as much superior to the angels as the name he has inherited is superior to theirs. For to which of the angels did God ever say, 'You are My Son. today I have become your Father?'"

Because of the strongly hierarchical culture of Bible times, names and titles were very important. This passage contrasts a son's status and a servant's. By native right Christ is God. He is divine and the angels are simply ministering spirits, as we read in Hebrews 1: 14: "Are not all angels ministering spirits sent to serve those who will inherit salvation?"

While Jesus is called the Son of God, angels are called servants—a vast difference in status. But before moving forward, we must confront another important problem. The word "Son" and the word "begotten" found in the King James translation of John 1:14

and other passages, can be confusing if misunderstood to mean that Christ—even though He is God—is inferior to the Father. Some teach this erroneous view even today.

The father-son relationship in Hebrew culture is very special, and God uses this relationship to express in human terms the relationship between Himself and Jesus Christ.

By calling Christ the Son of the Father, by no means does the writer mean that the Father produced the Son or that the Father is superior to the Son. Christ, as God, was one with the Father from eternity. May I remind you of Philippians 2:6. It was not robbery for Jesus to make Himself equal with the Father. He is of the very nature of God. A famous Christian writer says, "In Him (*Christ*), was life, original, unborrowed and underived." What a beautiful definition of Christ as the Son of God!

The word "begotten" can be misleading in that it suggests to some that the Father produced the Son. The problem here is that the English language has only one meaning for the word "begotten"—which is "produced". But the New Testament was not written in English, and the Greek of the New Testament uses a word quite distinctive in meaning from the King James Version's "only begotten son." The Greek words translated "only begotten" actually means "somebody unique or somebody special, one of a kind." The word translated here as "begotten,"standing alone, can indeed mean "to produce." But this meaning is never used for Christ in the New Testament. It applies only to human beings, for we are created beings; we have been produced. The meaning applied to Jesus is the first one—somebody unique, somebody special, one of a kind. When John says, "The Word was made flesh" he is dealing with a unique Person. Christ was fully God and fully man in one Person.

Christians argued about this question for more than 300 years. Finally, about 400 years after Christ, in one of its councils the Church accepted that Jesus was fully God and fully man because of His unique personality, which they could not explain but accepted as divine, biblical truth. It is a key doctrine of the Christian church today.

Both words, "Son" and "begotten" are used here to point out the fact that Christ is unique—that there is a very special Father-Son relationship. Neither of these terms ever implies that Jesus is inferior to the Father. Christ, as God, is equal with the Father. They are One in purpose, One in stature but, in the plan of salvation, Christ lowered Himself—emptied Himself—and became a Servant in order to be the Redeemer of the world.

Angels Worship Him

The second evidence of Christ's superiority is that the angels worship Him. Worship is an admission that the person or object of worship is superior to the worshipers.

By worshipping Christ, the angels admit that He is divine, since only divinity can be worshipped. Hebrews 1:6 reads: "And again, when God brings His firstborn into the world. . . ." Firstborn in this case means the Head, or First, of the plan of salvation. The verse concludes, "He (*God*) says, 'Let all God's angels worship Him.'"

In both Daniel and Revelation we read about thousands and thousands of angels worshipping Jesus Christ, the Son of God. This itself is clear evidence that He is not a mere human being, but divine.

John Bunyan, the great tinker of Bedford who we all know for his famous book, *Pilgrim's Progress*, writes: "If Jesus Christ is not God, then heaven will be filled with idolaters." What a beautiful statement! Bunyan is right; Jesus is God.

In the next verse (Hebrews 1:7) the writer says more about the angels, quoting Psalm 104:4: "He makes winds his messengers, flames of fire his servants." What does this mean? It means that while we humans have no real control over wind and fire (as we well know from hurricanes and wild fires that devastate the country), angels *can* control these elements. The angels, therefore, are superior to man. And by inference, since angels are superior to human beings and Christ is superior to angels, then Christ must be superior to mankind.

God's Word says clearly that only God is to be worshipped and that anyone who worships something or someone besides God is an idolater. When angels worship Christ, as mentioned in Hebrews 1:6, they prove that they regard Him as God.

In Revelation 19:10 John the Revelator begins worshipping the angel Gabriel because of the tremendous revelation the angel has brought: "I fell at his feet to worship him (*John worshipping Gabriel*) but he (*Gabriel*) said to me, 'Do not do it. I am a fellow servant with you and with your brothers who hold to the testimony of Jesus.'"

His Authority

Now we turn to the third reason for accepting Christ's superiority over the angels. The writer of Hebrews points to Christ as being superior to the angels on the basis of *authority.*

In both Old and New Testaments, the Bible describes angels as ministers of God. But ultimate authority belongs to God, and God Himself addresses Christ as divine.

Notice Hebrews 1:8: "But about the Son, he says, 'Your throne, O God, will last forever and ever, and righteousness will be the scepter of your kingdom.'" Clearly this is the Father speaking to the Son and saying, "Your throne, O God."

The writer of Hebrews is making clear that the Father not only addresses Christ as God and acknowledges Him as Creator, but above all is pleased with His saving mission on earth. He therefore confirms Christ's authority over the plan of salvation.

We read in Hebrews 1:9-14: "'You have loved righteousness and hated wickedness; therefore God, your God, has set you above your companions by anointing you with the oil of Joy.' He also says, 'In the beginning, O Lord, you laid the foundation of the earth and the heavens are the works of your hands.'"

In other words Christ is the Creator. John 1:3 makes it very clear: "Through him all things were made; without him nothing was made that has been made."

Hebrews 1:11 says: "They will perish (*creation will come to an end*) but you remain; they will wear out like a garment. You will roll them up like a robe; like a garment they will be changed. But you remain the same, and your years will never end."

This, of course, is pointing to Christ as God. In verse 13 Paul asks, "To which of the angels did God ever say, Sit at My right hand until I make your enemies a footstool for your feet? Are not all angels ministering spirits set to serve those who inherit salvation?"

Oh! the wonderful truth about Christ is that He is not simply above the angels, but as God He became man, and as man He became the Savior of the world.

The first person to see Jesus alive after His resurrection, interestingly enough, is Mary. She apparently takes hold of His ankle when she falls to worship Him, for Jesus says to her, "Mary, don't hold onto Me."

The King James Version reads, "Don't touch Me". But the actual Greek text says, "Don't cling to Me". We can assume, then, that she takes hold of Him and perhaps says, "I am not letting you go." That's how much Christ means to her. And Jesus says, "Mary, please don't hold onto Me. Don't cling to Me. I have not yet ascended to My Father and to your Father, to My God and to your God."

What is Jesus telling her? The New Testament—especially the Gospel of John and Galatians—explains the significance of Jesus' words. John 3:17 says, "For God did not send his Son into the world, to condemn the world but to save the world through him." Galatians 4: 4 and 5 tells us that in the fullness of time God sent His Son, made of a woman, made under the law to redeem us from under the law.

In the implementation of the plan of salvation, the Father becomes the Chairman. Jesus becomes the Savior and, of course, the Holy Spirit is the Communicator.

As Savior in human form, Jesus voluntarily places Himself under the authority of the Father. And after Jesus finishes His earthly mission, He needs His Father's approval so that He can deliver the Great Commission to His followers. So after the resurrection He goes back to the Father and receives that approval. The Father says to Him, "Son, Your act of redemption, Your perfect life, and Your sacrificial death fully satisfy the law on behalf of the human race that I sent You to redeem."

Once Jesus receives this validation, He comes back to earth and delivers the Great Commission to His disciples.

The well-known words of that Great Commission appear in Matthew 28:18 and 19: "Then Jesus came to them (*the disciples*) and said, 'All authority in heaven and on earth has been given to me.'" The King James says "all power", but the actual Greek word is "authority". The New International Version is absolutely correct in using the word "authority".

What does Jesus mean when He says, "all authority"? It clearly means all authority to take those who accept Him as their Savior to heaven: "All authority in heaven and on earth has been given to me. Therefore, go and make disciples of all nations, baptizing them in the name of the Father and of the Son and of the Holy Spirit, and teaching them to obey everything I have commanded you. And surely I am with you always, to the very end of the age."

We thank Jesus that even though He is by nature above the angels, He became one of us and was made lower than the angels to be the Savior of mankind.

To the Christian Jews of New Testament times, this evidence of Christ's superiority to the angels is most reassuring, especially as it pertains to their ultimate salvation. And the idea that Christ is now sitting at the right hand of God, the Father, interceding for His people until all their enemies are crushed, gives 21st-century believers blessed hope, too.

Pay Careful Attention

We must therefore take very seriously the appeal of Hebrews 2:1-4. It reads, "We must pay more careful attention, therefore, to what we have heard, so that we do not drift away (*give up our faith in Christ*). For if the message spoken by angels was binding, and every violation and disobedience received its just punishment, how shall we escape if we ignore such a great salvation? This salvation, which was first announced by the Lord, was confirmed to us by those who heard him. God also testified to it by signs, wonders, and various miracles, and gifts of the Holy Spirit distributed according to His will."

Christians cannot treat lightly the wonderful gift of salvation in Jesus Christ. Those who turn their backs on Christ are turning their backs on salvation. Christians, by definition, are citizens of heaven and as such look forward to Christ's Second Coming, when He will end all their struggles and take them to heaven, where He is now preparing a place for them.

But in the meantime they remain in Satan's territory—on enemy land. What concerns the writer of Hebrews most about Christians who read his epistle is that they not give up their faith in Christ. The *righteousness* that entitles them to heaven is always in Christ. That cannot be destroyed. But Satan *can* touch—he *can* destroy—the *faith* that dwells within. This is because righteousness comes by faith, and while all righteousness is in Christ, faith lies within His followers. Satan can indeed touch that faith, and Hebrews makes a powerful case for holding onto that faith in Christ.

Jesus Himself says in Matthew 10:17-22 that only those who endure to the end will be saved.

We end this study with the words of Matthew 10, spoken by the Lord, Jesus Christ to His disciples: "But be on your guard against men; they will hand you over to the local council and flog you in their synagogues. On My account you will be brought before governors and kings as witnesses to them and to the Gentiles. . . . All men will hate you because of me, but he who stands firm to the end, will be saved" (verses 17-22).

Jesus knows that persecution is coming and that His disciples' faith will be tested to the limit. So He warns them in advance, preparing them to stand in their time of trouble.

CHAPTER 3

Christ—God Who Exalted Man

Hebrews 2:5-13

So far in our study of the Epistle to the Hebrews, we have learned that this book contains the clearest presentation in all Scripture of the eternal mission of Jesus Christ.

In Hebrews 2 we have found one of the great Christological passages of the New Testament, and in verses 5-13 we will study the writer's description of how Christ, the Son of God, exalted mankind at His birth, during His life, at His death, and in His resurrection.

In our last study we saw how Hebrews points to Christ as greater than the angels—for Jesus is God. In this study we will look at the other side of Christ and see how He who by nature is greater than the angels was made a little lower than the angels so that He might exalt mankind above the angels. This is all part of the fantastic good news of the gospel.

Agape (ah-GAH-pay) Love

For Jesus to do what He did, as Son of God he had to become the Son of Man. To exalt mankind above the angels, He himself had to assume corporate humanity. He had to become part and parcel of the human race He came to redeem. In doing this Christ revealed one of the great qualities of God—His unconditional *agape (ah-GAH-pay)* love.

In 1 Corinthians 13:5 we are told that this *agape* love is the very nature of God. 1 John 4:8 and 16 tells us that God is Love and that this kind of love "seeketh not her own." It is self-emptying: "It is not self-seeking in terms of our personal ambitions."

Because of God's self-emptying love, He became a man in order to lift up the sinful human race and exalt above the angels those who accept His salvation. Last chapter we studied Philippians 2:6 and 7, which beautifully describes the love of God. In Philippians 2:6 we are told that Christ, as God, is equal with the Father. It is not robbery for Him to be considered equal with the Father, and yet in verse 7 we are told that He emptied Himself and became a servant in the likeness of men.

In 2 Corinthians 8:9 we find the same idea in different words—that Christ as God was *rich* but He became *poor* when He became one of us, that through that poverty we might become rich in Him—another way of presenting the wonderful news of salvation from a human point of view.

It is only in the context of this divine self-emptying love that we can begin to understand the unsearchable riches God has given through Christ and revealed in Hebrews 2.

Hebrews 2:5-13 beautifully describes the wonderful truth of how Christ, the Son of God, humbled Himself and became a man in order to exalt mankind.

We begin by reading the passage itself: "It is not to angels that he has subjected the world to come, about which we are speaking. But there is a place where someone has testified: 'What is man that you are mindful of him, the son of man that you care for him? You made him a little lower than the angels; you crowned him with glory and honor and put everything under his feet.' In putting everything under him, God left nothing that is not subject to him. Yet at the present we do not see everything subject to him. But we see Jesus, who was made a little lower than the angels, now crowned with glory and honor because he suffered death, so that by the grace of God he might taste death for everyone.

"In bringing many sons to glory, it was fitting that God, for whom and through whom everything exists, should make the author of their salvation perfect through suffering. Both the one who makes men holy and those who are made holy are of the same family. So Jesus is not ashamed to call them brothers. He says, 'I will declare your name to my brothers; in the presence of the congregation I will sing your praises.' And again, 'I will put my trust in him.' And again he says, 'Here am I and the children God has given me.'"

Hebrews 1 contrasts the angels with Christ, the Son of God. Now, beginning with Hebrews 2:5, the author contrasts angels with mankind. Angels will never rise to a higher position than they presently have, he says. The fallen angels will not be redeemed. Therefore, unfallen angels—angels that did not rebel with Lucifer against God—will never have the privilege of ruling the earth after it has been redeemed and made new.

Notice the future tense in "It is not to angels that he has subjected the world to come." This is the ultimate reality of salvation at the Second Coming of Christ.

The passage continues, "But there is a place where someone has testified: 'What is man that you are mindful of him, the son of man that you care for him? You made him a little lower than the angels; you crowned him with glory and honor and put everything under his feet.'"

God created mankind a little lower than the angels, and that is our position today. But one day, Paul tells us, mankind will be crowned with glory and honor to rule above the angels. Paul tells us, in fact, in the Epistle to the Corinthians that mankind will judge angels. God intends to exalt mankind, not only to rule this world made new but to be joint heirs with Christ and reign with Him throughout eternity. This is what Hebrews 2:6 and 8 is suggesting.

What does Paul mean with the phrase "in a certain place"? This "place" is Psalms 8:4, 6, and 7—a quote that says that mankind was given dominion over all the animals God created on earth. All the beasts of the field—everything—was placed under Adam, the father of the human race.

A Tale of Two Lions

An incident that happened to me in the mission filed helps me understand this passage. While I was in Uganda, a fellow missionary and I one day parked our car under a tree to have lunch and noticed that two lions were resting in its branches. The average lion in Africa weighs about 350 pounds and has such powerful front paws that it can break a man's neck with a single slap. Needless to say, the two of us remained in our vehicle as we watched the two lions and the lions watched us.

In most countries, lions like these are found only in cages, while people run free. In this instance, the opposite was true—we remained locked in my car while the lions enjoyed their freedom.

After we'd finished our lunches, I turned the ignition key to continue our journey, but the car refused to start. I knew that the only way to start the car was to get out, lift the hood, and press a reset button. But one of the lions was now lying on a branch only a few feet above where I would need to stand to press the button.

Since lions can smell fear in human beings, to relax myself I began giving the lion a Bible study as I got out of the car and lifted the hood to press the button. I preached from Psalm 8 and told the lion, "You may be stronger than I am, more powerful. You may be the king of the beasts, but I want you to know, dear lion, that God has given man dominion over all the beasts of the field, and that includes you."

The lion looked at me as if to say, "What are you doing in my territory?" But the Lord kept the lion there in the tree, and when I pressed the button and started the car, the lion twitched his tail—a signal that he was about to pounce. But just in time I climbed back into the car and we drove away.

Greater Dominion

The writer of Hebrews is saying here that man was given dominion over this world when it was first created. But Paul is now saying that God will one day crown redeemed humanity—those who have accepted the gift of salvation in Christ—with a glory greater than He gave Adam at creation. God intends to exalt His believers to be rulers of the universe.

The second half of Hebrews 2:8 says: "In putting everything under him, God left nothing that is not subject to him." How wonderful that we have a God who plans to make us joint heirs with Christ, above the angels—rulers of the universe with Christ. All this is God's purpose for us, through the redemption that is in Christ—though, as Paul says, "At present we do not see everything subject to Him."

Let me buttress this wonderful truth by quoting two other passages from the New Testament. The first is found in Romans 8:16 and 17, where Paul writes: "The Spirit himself testifies with our spirit that we are God's children. Now, if we are God's children, then we are heirs—heirs of God and co-heirs (*or joint heirs*) with Christ if indeed we share in his suffering in order that we may also share in his glory."

Remember that Hebrews tells us that Christ has already been glorified—though His followers have not. But Paul promises that one day that glorification will belong to those who hold fast their faith in Him who loved us and gave Himself for us.

The second promise is found in both Revelation 20:6 and Revelation 22:5 and tells us that those who have part in the first resurrection—that is, the believers—will reign with Christ 1,000 years in heaven and rule the universe forever with Christ when the earth is made new.

Never Give Up!

In this light, how foolish for anyone to give up his or her faith because of some problem or suffering. The writer of Hebrews is saying, basically: "Stop allowing your present circumstances to destroy your future hope in Christ."

This is his primary point in writing this Epistle to the wavering Jewish Christians in New Testament. Of course, the danger of losing their faith is not limited to them. Christians today face the same hazard.

In Hebrews 10:35 Paul says clearly, "Therefore do not cast away your confidence, which has great reward." He then adds in verse 38, "The just shall live by faith; But if anyone draws back, My soul has no pleasure in him" (NKJV).

Christians must never give up their faith in Christ, no matter what they are going through at the moment. In 1 John 3:1 and 2 we read: "How great is the love the Father has lavished on us, that we (*the believers*) should be called the children of God!"

The passage continues addressing believers who have accepted Christ as their personal Savior: "And what we will be has not yet been made known. But we know that when he appears, we shall be like him, for we shall see him like he is. Everyone who has this hope in him purifies himself, just as he is pure."

Christians must keep their eyes focused on that future, blessed hope they will experience when Christ comes the second time. Yes, they are already citizens of heaven, but they must remember that they are still living in enemy territory. The Prince of this World is still going about, roaring as a lion, trying to devour whomever he can (1 Peter 5:8). In this environment, Christians may indeed face suffering. Satan will do his very best to destroy their faith in Christ—through persecution, materialism, and by perverting the gospel.

Safeguarding Faith

Inspired writers, however, have written many promises to bolster faith when believers are attacked by the devil. Those being *persecuted* physically, mentally, or socially, can turn to Matthew 10:17-22 and James 1:2-4 for inspiration. When lured by *materialism* and the trinkets of this world, Christians should read Luke 21:34-36 and 1 Timothy 6:6-10.

And when tempted to *pervert the gospel* by regarding their own works as requirements for salvation, they should turn to Paul's Epistle to the Galatians and his second Epistle to the Corinthians—specifically Galatians 1:6 and 7, Galatians 5:4, and 2 Corinthians 11:3 and 4. These passages provide inspired safeguards against Satan's designs to destroy the Christian's faith in Christ.

We now turn to Hebrews 2:9, however, where Paul reminds his readers that they must constantly keep their eyes focused on Christ: "But we see Jesus, who was made a little lower than the angels, now crowned with glory and honor because he suffered death, so that by the grace of God he might taste death for everyone."

This death is not the temporary "sleep death" to which all Christians are subject in this world. The death spoken of here is what Revelation 20 calls the "second death"—the death that comes only when God ultimately abandons a sinner to the full wages of his sin. Because Christ suffered this penalty once and for all, faithful believers will be spared this penalty forever.

We must never forget how much Christ has suffered to exalt sinful humanity. By uniting Himself to corporate humanity in need of redemption, Christ was made perfect through suffering to save and exalt mankind. We must not limit that suffering to the cross alone. Yes, at the cross He went through extreme suffering—physical, mental, and spiritual. But Christ suffered throughout His life as he authored our salvation.

We read in Hebrews 2:10: "In bringing many sons to glory, it was fitting that God, for whom and through whom everything exists, should make the author of their salvation (*Jesus Christ*) perfect through suffering." Not only should this fill Christians' minds with deep gratitude and appreciation, their grateful hearts will be prepared to suffer in turn for Christ, while they await His return.

Acts 5:40-42 says that Christ's apostles were captured, flogged, and forbidden to preach by the local religious council (Sanhedrin). How did the Christians respond?: "The apostles left the Sanhedrin, rejoicing because they had been counted worthy of suffering disgrace for the Name. Day after day in the Temple courts and from house to house, they never stopped teaching and proclaiming the good news that Jesus is the Christ."

They were willing to suffer because they knew in whom they believed. They knew that in Jesus Christ they had salvation full and complete. One day they will have the experience of Hebrews 2:11-13, where Paul records: "Both the one who makes men holy and those who are made holy are of the same family. So Jesus is not ashamed to call them brothers. He says, 'I will declare your name to my brothers; in the presence of the congregation, I will sing your praises.' And again, 'I will put my trust in Him.' And again he says, 'Here am I and the children God has given me.'"

Jesus here declares His followers children of God. In light of this, how can they give up their blessed hope?

As we conclude this chapter of study, let us read the testimony and counsel of Paul in 2 Corinthians 4:16-18: "Therefore, we do not lose heart. Though outwardly we are wasting away, yet inwardly we are being renewed day by day. For our light and momentary troubles are achieving for us an eternal glory that far outweighs them all. So we fix our eyes, not on what is seen (*present circumstances*), but on what is unseen, (*the future hope in Christ*). For what is seen is temporary but what is unseen is eternal."

May God bless us in the truth that sets us free, that our faith in Christ may be unshakeable.

CHAPTER 4

God Suffers for Man

Hebrews 2:14-18

According to Hebrews 2, Christ, the Son of God, joined Himself to humanity and became the Son of Man for three main reasons.

We considered the first reason last study—that Jesus came to redeem man from his lost destiny and exalt him above the angels (Hebrews 2: 5-13). This He accomplished through His death and resurrection.

Now we will study the other two reasons Christ joined Himself to mankind's corporate humanity.

Release from Bondage

The second and third reasons Jesus joined Himself to humanity were to release mankind from its bondage through the fear of death and to become its merciful and faithful High Priest.

We find both spelled out in Hebrews 2:14-18, a passage full of meaning and well worth our careful study: "Since the children have flesh and blood, he too shared in their humanity so that by his death he might destroy him who holds the power of death—that is, the devil— and free those who all their lives were held in slavery by their fear of death. For surely, it is not angels he helps, but Abraham's descendants. For this reason he had to be made like his brothers in every way, in order that he might become a merciful and faithful high priest in service to God, and that he might make atonement for the sins of the people. Because he himself suffered when he was tempted, he is able to help those who are being tempted." What a tremendous passage!

As we begin to study the passage in detail, we must remember that last study we touched on Christ's becoming a little lower than the angels to pay the infinite price for our sins on the cross and exalt humanity above the angels.

Now in this passage, the writer of Hebrews reminds his readers that the humanity Christ assumed at the incarnation was the very same humanity with which they were born.

Fear of Death

Another important reason Christ became one with humanity was to deliver it from the universal bondage of the fear of death, under Satan's rule, as verses 14 and 15 show.

A hospital nurse once told me that every baby is born with a powerful fear of being dropped. From the baby's point of view, being dropped means death. Only later does it discover that there are many other ways of dying. If anything, the fear of death only intensifies with age.

That is the human predicament. We are born slaves to the fear of death—which explains why there are no atheists in foxholes. No sane man or woman is comfortable with dying.

Paul says that because of Adam's sin death reigned over mankind (Romans 5:17). Nothing we can do in and of ourselves offers an escape from the inevitability of death that comes as a result of Adam's fall. But one of the three big reasons Jesus came and joined Himself to mankind was to liberate us from the fear of death.

The Jews to whom Paul was writing were very familiar with the Old Testament—especially the first five books of the Old Testament, known as the Torah or Book of the Law. They knew that the Torah teaches that an innocent person cannot be punished for the guilty. Neither guilt nor righteousness is transferable from one person to another. The law simply does not allow it. Deuteronomy 24:16, for example, clearly says that a father cannot be punished for his son; Ezekiel 18:21 describes the same issue. That guilt and punishment cannot be transferred is a fundamental principle of biblical law.

Legally Guilty

So, to qualify as mankind's Savior, Jesus had to become part of guilty humanity. To legally save mankind from the condemnation of the law, Christ had to become a man with a condemned human nature. But we must be very careful. This does not make Christ a sinner. In becoming human, He was assuming something that was ours—not His—by native right. This is why the New Testament always adds a qualifying word when discussing the humanity of Christ.

John 1:14 says, "Christ was made flesh."

Galatians 4:4 and 5 reads, "Christ was made of a woman, made under the law."

2 Corinthians 5:21 teaches that "Christ was made to be sin."

The word *"made"* indicates that He became something that really was not His by nature. He was God by right. He was holy. He was righteous. But He *assumed* our humanity. When He became one of us, He assumed everything that we are under the law, under its curse, under its condemnation, so that He might redeem humanity from all these things.

This is why Christ is called the second, or last, Adam. The word "Adam" in Hebrew means mankind. When Christ united Himself with humanity, He became its Second Adam. Then, and only then, was He legally qualified to be our Substitute and Representative. This substitution in and of itself did not save humanity—but it did legally qualify Jesus to be our Savior.

Having become one of us in the incarnation and having obeyed the law in every detail, He met the positive demands of the law by His perfect obedience for 33 years. Then He took that corporate humanity to the cross and met the justice of the law. He surrendered to the wages of sin, and thus, by His perfect life and sacrificial death, He rewrote the history of the human race and changed its status from condemnation to justification.

Paul states this beautifully in Romans 5:18: "Consequently, just as the result of one trespass was condemnation for all men, so also the result of one act of righteousness was justification that brings life for all men." This does not mean that all men will go to heaven. Like any gift, God's supreme gift must be accepted. We cannot enjoy a gift we refuse to accept. Jesus makes it very clear in John 3:18 that the only reason anyone will be lost is because they purposely, persistently, and ultimately reject the good news of salvation.

Paul is telling us that in becoming one of us, in dying on the cross, Jesus redeemed us from the curse of the law, "having been made a curse for us" (Galatians 3:13).

In doing this Jesus also rescued humanity from enslavement to the fear of death. On the cross Christ abolished the second death and in its place provided His own immortal life.

The Great Exchange

Two things took place at the cross—a Great Exchange occurred. First, humanity's life, which Christ assumed, came to an end—not just for three days but forever. But in exchange, because God so loved the world, He gave humanity the eternal life of His Son. We repeat John 3:16 so often, yet we fail to ask exactly what Jesus means when He says that God gave His only begotten Son.

John explains this wonderful gift in 1 John 5:11,12. "And this is the testimony (*the record*): God has given us eternal life, and this life is in his Son. He who has the Son has life (*eternal life*); he who does not have the Son of God (*he who rejects this Gift*) does not have life (*eternal life*)."

The two things that took place at the cross during this Great Exchange are beautifully expressed by the apostle Paul when he writes to Timothy. Paul is in prison. He is about to be executed. He's concerned about who will carry on the great ministry of proclaiming and defending the gospel. He chooses Timothy and writes him one of his last letters before his death.

In 2 Timothy 1:8-10 he says: "So, do not be ashamed to testify about our Lord, or ashamed of me, his prisoner. But join with me in suffering for the gospel, by the power of God, who has saved us and called us to a holy life—not because of anything we have done but because of his own purpose and grace. This grace was given us in Christ Jesus before the beginning of time." Here Paul is referring to the plan of salvation made by God even before He created Adam.

In verse 10 Paul presents the reality: "But it has now been revealed (*it has become a historical fact*) through the appearing of our Savior, Christ Jesus, who has destroyed death (*not the first or sleep death which we Christians also have to experience but the second death*) and has brought life and immortality to light through the gospel."

Condemnation Nailed to the Cross

So, on the cross, two things took place. First, humanity's condemned life was executed once and for all. This is what Jesus means in John 12:30 and 31: "Now is the time for judgment on this world; now the prince of this world will be driven out. But I, when I am lifted up from the earth, will draw all men to myself." The "now" refers to the cross and "the world" refers to the human race. The humanity of Christ was not only just like ours, it included us. We were in Christ. The central theme of Paul's theology is this "in Christ" idea. Humanity was in Christ (its Creator) when He died on the cross, and 2 Corinthians 5:14 makes this very clear. "One died for all, and therefore all died."

On the cross the wages of sin was paid in Jesus Christ so that mankind will never have to suffer that kind of death. By doing that, He freed humanity from the fear of the second death, the wages of sin. This is the wonderful gift of God.

Jesus says, "Peace I leave with you, the peace that the world cannot give you, the peace that passes understanding." In 1 John 4:16-18 we read: "And so we know and rely on the love God has for us." Notice that it is not about humanity's love for God but God's love for humanity. God is Love—self-emptying, unconditional Love. "God is love. Whoever lives in love lives in God, and God in him. In this way, love is made complete (*perfect*) among us so that we will have confidence on the day of judgment, because in this world, we are like him."

True Christians have no fear of the judgment because Christ is on their side. God looks at them as if they were Jesus: "There is no fear in love. But perfect love drives out fear, because fear has to do with punishment. The one who fears is not made perfect in love."

Christians need to be made perfect in love so that they can be liberated from the fear of the wages of sin. Once they are liberated from this fear through their faith in Jesus Christ, why should they give up their hope? This is Paul's argument.

Faithful High Priest

Now we come to the third reason why Christ became a man—to be a faithful and merciful High Priest. By taking humanity to Himself and fully redeeming them from the sin problem, Jesus Christ becomes their Savior. But much more than that, He exalted redeemed humanity above the angels. Not only did He deliver humanity from the wages of sin, He now sits at the right hand of God as a great High Priest. Hebrews 2:16-18 clearly says: "For surely, it is not angels he helps but Abraham's descendants. For this reason he had to be made like his brothers in every way, in order that he might become a merciful and faithful high priest in service to God, and that he might make atonement for the sins of the people. Because he himself suffered when he was tempted, he is able to help those who are being tempted."

Hebrews 5:1 tells us that one of the qualifications for Christ—or anyone—to be a High Priest is that He must be chosen from among men if he is to represent them. For Christ to qualify as humanity's High Priest, He had to join humanity so that no one could ever accuse him of not representing humanity with mercy and understanding. Being one with humanity, He understands our struggles. He understands what we experience. He can sympathize with us but, more than that, He can help His followers in their battle against the flesh—against their sinful natures.

This is where the law of God and Christ part company. Yes, God's law and God Himself are similar in that both are holy and righteous. But they differ in that while God in Christ is capable of sympathizing with mankind's weakness and helping with its struggles, the law is incapable of empathizing with our plight. Nor is the law capable of helping humanity in its battles against sin. Under the law, then, no one can save themselves. Only under grace is there hope, for humanity has a Savior under grace who not only conquered and condemned sin in the flesh (Romans 8:3), but is able both to sympathize with human weakness and help His followers in their walk. This wonderful High Priest sits at the right hand of God, interceding for mankind.

Notice in Hebrews 2:18 what Paul says about Christ's sufferings: "Because he himself suffered when he was tempted." Christ suffered while being tempted, as the King James Version says. We know from Hebrews 4:15 that Christ was tempted in all points. This does not mean He was tried with every single temptation that has ever come to mankind. This would be impossible. He could not, for example, be tempted to overindulge in television viewing. TV did not exist in His day. But He was tempted in all the *basic* drives in which all humans are tempted.

According to 1 John 2:15,16, the three basic drives in which all are tempted are the lust of the flesh, the lust of the eyes, and the pride of life. The lust of the flesh is a natural, but now sinfully perverted, desire with which God created mankind. The lust of the eyes is covetousness, as in "we want what we see." The pride of life means that we want to be Number One. Man is always trying to be first, and those who fail to achieve that status develop low self esteem because of their failure.

But Hebrews 2:18 says Jesus suffered, and we must ask, "Where did He suffer?" Clearly he suffered while subjected to temptation—not only on the cross itself. The answer as to where He suffered is clearly revealed in 1 Peter 4:1: "Therefore since Christ suffered in his body (*his flesh*), arm yourselves also with the same (*mind* in KJV) attitude, because he who has suffered in his body (*or flesh*) is done with sin (*has ceased from sin* in KJV)."

In other words the mind of Christ was controlled by the Holy Spirit, but His nature (which was human) was controlled by the principle of self—the law of sin. But Christ never allowed His flesh to have a say in its desires. For every temptation that came to Christ, through the power of the Holy Spirit his mind said, "No." And thus the flesh was deprived of its desire to serve self.

One of the greatest temptations for Christ, for example, was to use His divine power for His own personal benefit—to turn stones into bread or to come down from the cross and save Himself. But in all this Jesus was victorious. He was tempted as we are, but He never gave in. Having overcome temptation and redeemed humanity, He returned to heaven to represent humanity as a great, faithful, and merciful High Priest.

We must never limit the suffering of Christ to those six hours on the cross—terrible as that experience was for Him. All through His earthly life, Christ deprived His assumed humanity of its desire to self-serve. Only in this way could He meet the positive demands of the law on behalf of fallen man. Having perfectly obeyed the law through the suffering of the flesh, Christ took that condemned flesh to the cross and surrendered it to the wages of sin. It was executed so that by His life and death, He could redeem mankind. He took a glorified, redeemed form of humanity to heaven. He will bestow this redeemed humanity on those He comes to take home at His Second Coming. But for now He uses his own redeemed form of humanity to represent humanity against the accusations of the devil (See Philippians 3:20,21).

No wonder Paul could write so graciously to the Corinthian Christians, "Thanks be to God for his indescribable gift" (2 Corinthians 9:15). May this be our attitude too.

CHAPTER 5
Christ—Greater than Moses
Hebrews 3:1-6

In our study of Hebrews 2:14-18 last chapter, we found that Christ became a man for three main reasons.

First, He came to recapture and restore mankind's lost destiny. Sin had placed all humankind under Satan's dominion. The whole world lay under the Evil One, says the apostle John in 1 John 5:19. Christ assumed human form to redeem mankind from that situation.

In Luke 11:20-22, for example, Jesus says to the Jews: "If I drive out demons by the finger of God, then the kingdom of God has come to you." Then He shares a parable: "When a strong man, fully armed, guards his own house, his possessions are safe." The "strong man" represents Satan, guarding his house (the human race) which he took captive through Adam. Jesus then continues, "But when someone stronger attacks and overpowers him, he takes away the armor in which the man trusted and divides up the spoils." Jesus is referring, of course, to Himself as the Great Redeemer of mankind.

The second reason Christ became a man was to release mankind from its bondage to sin and fear of death. Adam's sin not only condemned *Adam* to death. Because all humanity was contained *in* him (biologically and spiritually), his sin brought condemnation upon the whole world. Romans 5:18 tells us that by one man's disobedience, condemnation came unto all men. First Corinthians 15:21 and 22 says that all are in Adam and all die. Humanity is thereby enslaved to the fear of death. But the wonderful good news is that God's love in Christ liberates them from this fear of the wages of sin—that is, death. So we read in 1 John 4:18, "Perfect love (*God's love*) casts out fear."

The third reason Christ became a man was to enable Him to become a faithful and merciful High Priest. In His human state, Christ by His life and death faithfully redeemed mankind from every aspect of sin. He thereby earned the right to legally represent mankind in the heavenly sanctuary as High Priest. He is merciful because He understands human weakness and struggles with the flesh. He was tempted in all points as human beings are tempted, according to Hebrews 4:15. But He conquered sin and therefore is able to sympathize with humanity. He is also able to help mankind in its struggles, as Paul explains in Hebrews 3:1-6.

Hebrews 3:1-6 Overview

Before we study Hebrews 3:1-6 in detail, however, let us read Paul's words just as they are written: "Therefore, holy brothers, who shared in the heavenly calling, fix your thoughts on Jesus, the Apostle and High Priest whom we confess. He was faithful to the one who appointed Him, just as Moses was faithful in all God's house. Jesus has been found worthy of greater honor than Moses just as the builder of a house has greater honor than the house itself. For every house is built by someone but God is the builder of everything. Moses was faithful as a servant in all God's house testifying to what would be said in the future but Christ is faithful as a Son over God's house. And we are His house if we hold on to our courage and the hope of which we boast." What a beautiful statement about Christ's faithfulness and what it means to us.

Holy Brothers?

In verse 1 we must consider three facts. First, Paul addresses the believers to whom he writes as "holy brothers." What does he mean, "holy brothers who shared in the holy calling"?

When Christians look at themselves, they see unholiness. But the good news in Ephesians 1:4 is that God chose them in Christ from the foundation of the world that they might be holy and without blame. This is why the New Testament addresses Christians as saints, not because they are saints in and of themselves, but saints in Christ. They have been sanctified in Christ. Even the Christians in Corinth—one of the worst churches in terms of behavior—were called saints (1 Corinthians 1:2).

First Corinthians 6:9-11 tells that group of erring Christians that they have been washed, justified, and sanctified in Christ. In Hebrews 10:14 we then read that by one sacrifice Christ has perfected forever those who are being sanctified. Christians are declared holy in Christ. This is very comforting and reassuring, for as true Christians look at themselves, they see nothing but sin.

Jesus, an Apostle

The second statement in Hebrews 3:1 admonishes us to fix our eyes on Jesus, the Apostle. The word "apostle" means "sent one," who lays the foundation or beginning of something. Christ, of course, is the One who laid the foundation. Ephesians 2:19 and 20 says: "Consequently, you are no longer foreigners and aliens." Paul is addressing the Gentile believers in Ephesus: "But fellow citizens with God's people (*the Jews who believed*) and members of God's household, built on the foundation of the apostle and prophets with Christ Jesus himself the chief cornerstone."

Those who live in Bible lands do not build with wood—termites pose too great a problem. They build, instead, with stone, and everything is measured from the cornerstone. Jesus the Cornerstone, therefore, is the Source of salvation.

Finally we read in Hebrews 3:1: "Fix your thoughts on Jesus, our High Priest whom we confess." A priest is the opposite of a prophet. A prophet represents God before the congregation; a priest, on the other hand, represents a congregation before God. When Christ went to heaven, He took a redeemed human nature with Him and now represents us. Not only is He now our perfect Savior, He is a faithful and merciful High Priest.

Moving on to Hebrews 3:2, we read: "He was faithful to the One who appointed Him just as Moses was faithful in all God's house." In what was Christ faithful to the One who appointed Him? Let's study together to find the answer.

In the plan of redemption, the Father takes the position of the Chairperson. He is the Director of the plan of salvation. He so loved the world that He sent His Son to redeem the world.

In John 3:17 we read that God sent His Son to the world, not to condemn it, but that through Him the world might be saved. In Paul's Epistle to the Galatians 4:4 and 5 we then find that "when the fullness of time had come, God sent His Son, made of a woman, made under the law, to redeem us from under the law." In this mission Jesus was faithful. It is for this reason, when He prayed to the Father in John 17:4, that He tells the Father that He has finished the work given Him to do. On the cross He cried out, "It is finished!" (John 19:30).

We are told in Philippians 2:6-8 that Christ was equal to God but that He emptied Himself. He made Himself of no reputation and became totally subject to the Father, as a slave to his master. Then He became obedient even to the death of the cross. Jesus was absolutely faithful to the mission that God sent Him here to accomplish—to redeem every human being.

This faithfulness is compared to Moses', who was a type of Christ. We read of the faithfulness of Moses in Exodus 32:9-13, 31, and 32. When Moses goes up the mountain, God gives him the Ten Commandments. But when Moses comes down and finds the people worshipping a golden calf, he throws the tables of stone to the ground, shattering them. He then goes back up the mountain, where God tells him to stand to one side while He wipes out the people who have rebelled against Him. In turn God promises to make a great nation from Moses' descendents.

Moses replies, in so many words, "God, please forgive these people, even though they have rebelled against You and me. If you cannot forgive them, then blot me out of the Book of Life that they may live in my place." Here we get a glimpse of God's character as reflected in the attitude of Moses, who was a type of Christ.

Greater than Moses

Hebrews 3:3 and 4 presents Christ's faithfulness as greater than Moses' faithfulness. God did not destroy Moses to save the Jews, for Moses was only a type of Christ. Though Moses was willing to be removed from the Book of Life and banned from heaven so that his people might live, he did not actually die for them. Christ, however, was faithful to the very end. He was obedient even unto death—the death of the cross—and because of this is presented as greater than Moses, just as the house owner is superior to the house itself.

Paul tells us in Hebrews 3: 3 and 4: "Jesus has been found worthy of greater honor than Moses, just as the builder of a house has greater honor than the house itself. For every house is built by someone, but God is the builder of everything."

Though Moses was highly regarded by the Jews, says Paul, Moses was only a type of the Messiah. True, Moses said he was willing to die the wages of sin, eternal death, for the salvation of the Jewish people. But he did not die for them, for he was not qualified to be the Messiah. He was only a type.

Christ, the Real Savior

But Christ is the reality! He tasted the wages of sin—the God-abandoned death—for humanity. "By the grace of God, Jesus tasted death for everyone," says Hebrews 2:9. This makes Him far superior to Moses.

In Hebrews 3:5 and 6, Paul again reminds his Jewish readers that Christ is superior to Moses, comparing Moses to a servant who points to the Messiah to come. In contrast, Christ Himself is the Son of God. He is the reality over the house of God, just as an earthly son often takes over the house that once belonged to his father. In these verses, both Moses and Christ are presented as being faithful. Christ, however, is portrayed as far superior, since Moses was the type but Christ is the reality of salvation.

In concluding our study we read verses 5 and 6, "Moses was faithful as a servant in all God's house, testifying to what would be said in the future. But Christ is faithful as a Son over God's house and we are his house, if we hold onto our courage and the hope of which we boast."

Notice that Paul says here that the believers make up Jesus' house. The word "house" refers to the church, the body of Christ. The writer of Hebrews is contrasting Moses with Christ, pointing out to Jewish believers to whom this letter was initially written, that Christ is far superior to Moses, as Savior. For Moses represents the law, which can save no one.

Romans 3:20 says that by the works of the law shall no flesh be justified. Paul repeats this three times in Galatians 2:16—that by the works of the law no human being will be justified. Salvation comes only through faith in Jesus Christ. While Christ—who saves sinners—is the fulfillment of Moses' law which God gave to the Jews, this law cannot save the believer, for it demands perfect obedience, rendered continually without one flaw. None can render such obedience except One—the Lord, Jesus Christ.

We find in Romans 10 a wonderful statement in which Paul contrasts salvation by faith in Jesus Christ with salvation by the works of the law. Paul is addressing the Jews in this passage, but his message also applies to us. Romans 10:4 says: "Christ is the end (*completion*) of the law so that there may be righteousness for everyone who believes."

In Jesus Christ the law was perfectly satisfied. By His life He met the positive demands of the law. By His death He met the justice of the law.

By His doing and His dying, Jesus established the law. In Romans 3 Paul asks the question, "Do we nullify the law by preaching justification by faith?"

He answers without a pause, "God forbid! Certainly not!" because through the life and death of Jesus Christ the law was established. Christ is the completion—the end—of the law for righteousness to everyone who believes.

In Romans 10:5 we discover what it means to be under the law: "Moses described in this way, the righteousness that is by the law. The man who does these things, will live by them." If we want to be saved through the law, it is not enough to believe in the law or to know the law. We have to keep it in every respect. We know that only Christ has done this.

Salvation in Christ is meaningful only to those who hold onto their faith in Him and do not give up. One of the major problems faced by the early Christians was the danger of reverting to Judaism.

Again, we must remember that the word "house" in Hebrews 3 has nothing to do with a structure or physical building but refers to the people—the household—of God.

Paul is saying that Christians are the true house of God. He presents the same idea in Ephesians 2:19-22, where he portrays Christ as the chief cornerstone on which the whole house stands.

Three Lessons

This study teaches us three important lessons. First, we must always remember that salvation is founded and grounded in Christ's faithfulness—not our own. In John 13:1 we read that He was faithful even unto death. He did not give up. He completely fulfilled the mission God sent Him here to accomplish.

When Jesus was about to leave for heaven, after finishing His earthly mission, He told His disciples: "All authority is given to Me. Therefore, go and make disciples of all nations, baptizing them in the name of the Father, the Son and the Holy Ghost" (Matthew 28:18,19).

We read in 1 Thessalonians 5:24: "Faithful is He that called you who will also do it." We must always remember that salvation is founded and grounded in Christ's faithfulness. For this believers thank God, for they have failed Him many times. But the Savior and High Priest never fails.

The second lesson is that Christ never disappoints His followers. In view of this, the believers' faith must never waver. Hebrews 10:35-39 tells us not to give up our confidence in Christ because "the just shall live by faith."

Paul raises the question in Romans 8:35, "Who will separate us from the love of God?" He answers his own question: Nothing, not persecution, famine, peril, the devil, or anything that is in heaven or earth can separate the believers from Jesus. As they remain rooted and grounded in the love of God, revealed in Jesus Christ by His life and, especially by His death on the cross, they enjoy an eternal bond with Him.

The third lesson is that the believers must respond positively to God's leadership. Israel murmured against Moses, making his life miserable, and many Jews who were delivered from Egypt never entered the Promised Land. They died in the wilderness because of unbelief (Hebrews 3:19).

Paul tells us in 1 Corinthians 10:11,12 that their history was recorded for the benefit of all believers, upon whom the ends of the world have come. Christians must be careful not make the same mistake.

Simply becoming a Christian is not enough—the believers' faith must endure to the end. In Matthew 10:17-22 Jesus tells His disciples that they will be persecuted, taken to court, and mistreated and will go through many difficult problems and trials. When such experiences come, something can happen inside that devastates, as faith and feelings part company.

Their feelings say that God has forsaken them—that they will never be able to go on and that they are not good enough to be saved. But faith cannot rest on one's performance or one's opinion of themselves. Their faith must rest in Christ's faithfulness. They must be able to say with Paul, "I know in whom I believe and He is able to save me to the uttermost because I come to God through Him" (See Hebrews 7:25).

Jesus ends this passage with these words: "He that is faithful to the end, will be saved." The Christian's faith must endure to the end and be founded on two things—the faithfulness of Christ as Savior and a High Priest who will never fail or forsake His people. He made it clear to His disciples and says today, "I will be with you to the end of the world" (See Mathew 28:20).

Christ is presented in Hebrews 3, not only as a perfect Savior who has redeemed His followers from every aspect of sin but as their Representative and High Priest. Jesus Christ is at the right hand of God, interceding against the accusations of Satan. He will one day come to take them home. But until then, they must be faithful to Him who is their Savior and High Priest. Their faith must endure to the end.

CHAPTER 6

Warnings from Israel's History
Hebrews 3:7 -19

In our last study we covered Hebrews 3:1-6—six verses in which the writer of Hebrews reveals two important facts that we should review before we study the remaining of the chapter.

We believe the writer of Hebrews to be Paul, and in the first six verses of Hebrews he makes these two important points: First, both Moses (who liberated the Jews from bondage in Egypt) and Christ (who redeemed humanity from the bondage of sin) were faithful in their missions. Moses was faithful in delivering the Jews from their Egyptian bondage; Christ was faithful in delivering humanity from its bondage to sin.

Paul's second point is that Christ is definitely the better of the two, since Moses is only a "type" of deliverer that Christ became in reality.

Two-way Faithfulness

Paul also discusses Israel's response to Moses in the Exodus. Moses was faithful in doing what God had called Him to do. But was Israel faithful to Moses? No. Faithfulness is a two-way street. While Moses was faithful to the mission God had given him, most adult Jews who left Egypt, delivered from the house of bondage, did not reach Canaan. They died in the wilderness.

Paul uses this historical fact to warn Jewish believers of his day— and by extension Christians today—that if they follow the Old Testament Jews' example, they will too die in the wilderness of unbelief. They will not enter the heavenly Canaan.

This passage emphasizes that belief in Christ—faith—must endure to the end if the believers are finally to enter the heavenly Canaan.

More Lessons from Exodus

We now turn to Hebrews 3:7-19 itself: "As the Holy Spirit says, Today, if you hear his voice, do not harden your hearts as you did in the rebellion, during the time of testing in the desert where your fathers tested and tried me and saw what I did. That is why I was angry with that generation and I said, Their hearts are always going astray and they have not known my ways. So I declared on an oath in my anger, They shall never enter my rest. See to it, brothers, that none of you has a sinful, unbelieving heart that turns away from the living God. But encourage one another daily, as long as it is called Today, so that none of you may be hardened by sin's deceitfulness. We have come to share in Christ if we hold firmly to the end the confidence we had at first. As it has just been said, today, if you hear his voice, do not harden your hearts as you did in the rebellion. Who are they who heard and rebelled? Were they not all those Moses led out of Egypt? And with whom was he angry for forty years? Was it not with those who sinned, whose bodies fell in the desert? And to whom did God swear that they would never enter his rest not to those who disobeyed? So we see that they were not able to enter because of their unbelief."

In Hebrews 3:6 Paul compares the church to a house. He reminds his readers that while Christ, like Moses, is faithful in His mission of saving His people, His hands are tied if they give up their faith in Him. Many Christians believe today that "once saved, always saved". But the Bible teaches no such thing. It does teach that as long believers hold fast to their faith, their salvation is guaranteed. But if they say good-bye to Christ in unbelief, they are also saying good-bye to the Source of their salvation.

God is sovereign. But He has given complete freedom of choice to His subjects, within that sovereignty. God created mankind with free will, and He cannot force heaven on those who voluntarily turn their backs on Christ. Unbelief ties a loving God's hands. Ultimate salvation can only be realized as believers hold fast to the hope of which they boast—their salvation in Christ. Jesus makes this point clear in Matthew 10:17-22. Only those who endure to the end will be saved.

The Epistle to the Hebrews clearly points out that it is not enough to believe at the beginning. Faith must endure to the end. Hebrews 10: 35-39 says: "So do not throw away your confidence (in Christ), it will be richly rewarded. You need to persevere so that when you have done the will of God, you will receive what he has promised. For in just a very little while, He who is coming, will come and will not delay. But my righteous one will live by faith (*He that is just by faith, will live*). And if he shrinks back, I (*God*) will not be pleased with him."

Next comes a reflective statement: "But, we are not of those who shrink back and are destroyed but of those who believe and are saved." Faith must endure to the end!

Under inspiration, Paul is using the unbelieving Jews of the Exodus as a warning to the Jewish Christians of the New Testament and by extension to all believers. Gentiles are no different than Jews. All are of the same nature and are in the same situation. The devil is doing everything he can to take the believers out of Christ. Christians must be on guard. Paul here retells the history of Israel to help his readers avoid Israel's mistakes. Hebrews 3:7-11 says: "So, as the Holy Spirit says (*convicts*): Today, if you hear his voice, do not harden your hearts as you did in the rebellion, during the time of testing in the desert, when your fathers tested and tried me and for forty years saw what I did. That is why I was angry with that generation, and I said, 'Their hearts were always going astray, and they have not known my ways.' So I declared on an oath in my anger, They shall never enter my rest."

This is the tragedy of many Christians. They begin well but shipwreck on the rocks of unbelief. In the parable of the sower, some seeds fall on thorny ground, some on poor soil. None of these reach maturity. Only those that fall onto good ground bear fruit. As long as the believers' hearts are controlled by the Holy Spirit through faith, they have hope and assurance. But if they allow their hearts to turn against Jesus Christ and salvation in Him, they lose salvation and suffer the "wrath" of God.

What is this "wrath" of God? Paul describes it in Romans 1:18-32. God's wrath is passive. He allows those who turn their backs to Him to suffer the consequences of their rejection, for He has created them with free will. Three times in this passage we read that God "gave up" those who deliberately, persistently, and ultimately rejected Him.

Isaiah 55:8 and 9 says: "For my thoughts are not your thoughts, neither are your ways my ways, declares the Lord. As the heavens are higher than the earth, so are my ways higher than your ways and my thoughts than your thoughts" (Isaiah 55:9). Our anger is active; God's wrath is passive. We must never project human concepts of anger onto God. When God says, "I am angry". He simply means that His hands are tied. He cannot give us what He has promised us in Christ if we turn our backs to Him, for He has created us with free will.

With this understanding of God's wrath, we now see that those who turn their backs on God can never enter God's "rest", or heaven. This is not because God has chosen them to be lost, but because they themselves have made this choice. The great majority of the Jews who were delivered from Egyptian bondage never arrived in Canaan because they hardened their hearts toward God. We must learn from their mistakes—this is the whole point of Paul's discourse in Hebrews 3, especially verse 12 onward which reads: "See to it brothers, that none of you has a sinful, unbelieving heart that turns away from the living God."

In verses 13 and 14, then, Paul admonishes his readers that if they see any of their fellow believers' faith dwindling, they must come to their aid before it is too late. We need to help each other in the Christian walk. Salvation and rest in Christ is guaranteed only as long as faith endures to the end.

True, faith does not save—it is the righteousness of Christ *through faith* that saves. It is His perfect life and sacrificial death that qualifies humanity for heaven. But salvation is made effective, individually, only by faith. Though Jesus died for all mankind—this the Bible clearly teaches—God created the human race with a free will. Humans can still choose to be lost. Without this understanding, we would have to teach the heresy of Universalism—that all mankind will someday be in heaven. Yet the Bible clearly says that not everyone will be in heaven—not because God has predestined some to be lost, but because some deliberately and unequivocally reject the gift of Jesus Christ, the Supreme Sacrifice that would otherwise qualify them for heaven.

The plea of this passage in Hebrews 3, therefore, is to never give up the faith. Salvation is guaranteed only as the believer rests in the righteousness of Christ by faith. This must be the major concern as God's people face the future and its problems. We are living in a time when Satan has come like a flood. He has made life difficult for many Christians. He wants to destroy the believers' faith. So Christians must help one another if they see faith dwindling among their fellow believers.

As he concludes Hebrews 3, Paul gives good advice in verses 14-19: "We have come to share in Christ if we hold firmly till the end the confidence we had at first."

Here Paul is saying that faith must endure, adding: "As has just been said: Today, if you hear his voice, do not harden your hearts as you did in the rebellion (*referring to the Exodus*). Who were they who heard and rebelled? Were they not all those whom Moses led out of Egypt?"

Paul is not referring to the unbelievers but to God's people who were delivered from Egypt, the house of bondage. In spite of the abundance of evidence and miracles God gave them during their 40 years of wilderness travel, they turned their backs on Him. As a result, Hebrews 3:19 says, "So we see that they were not able to enter, because of their unbelief."

According to the first half of 1 Corinthians 10, which uses the Exodus as a type of salvation, Paul says that Moses is a type of Christ. Crossing the Red Sea is a type of baptism. Pharaoh signifies a type of Satan, while Egypt represents the world. When the Jews of the Exodus crossed the Red Sea, they turned away from Egypt and Pharaoh physically. But their hearts, unfortunately, were still in Egypt. This was the stumbling block that prevented them from entering the Promised Land.

Some Christians today want to have one leg in the church and one leg in the world. They must make a choice! It is either the world or the church. It is either Satan or Christ. Jesus—the God-man Savior or Satan, the angel Lucifer turned rebel. Both are battling for the souls of men.

Although the Jews crossed the Red Sea physically, their hearts were still back in Egypt. They complained repeatedly that they wished they were back in Egypt, for they missed the leeks and onions. Christians must be careful that the things of the world do not pull them out of Christ. The greatest hazard Christians face today is the battle of faith.

As Paul neared the end of his life, he wrote to Timothy in 2 Timothy 4:7,8: "I have fought the good fight. I have finished the race. And now there is a crown of righteousness waiting for me, and not only for me but for all those who love his appearing."

The formula for salvation and Christian living is one and the same: "Not I, but Christ." (Galatians 2:20). This is righteousness by faith.

For 40 years unbelief, murmuring, and rebellion shut out ancient Israel from the land of Canaan. The same sins have delayed many modern Christians from entering the heavenly Canaan. In neither case are God's promises at fault. It is unbelief, worldliness, lack of consecration, and strife among the Lord's professed people that have kept them in this world of sin and sorrow so many years.

Many Christians who began well come to disaster because their faith dwindles and they at last turn their backs on God. Six months before Christ came on the scene, God sent John the Baptist to prepare the way for Him. Many responded to the preaching of John, repented, and were baptized. But only months later, many of those same people turned their backs on Christ. What happened? They allowed the things of this world to undermine their faith.

When Christians accept Christ, they change their citizenship from the world to heaven. They remove their allegiance from Satan and give it to Christ. Christ becomes not only their Savior but their Lord and Master. But they are still living in enemy territory. Satan is still going about like a roaring lion, seeking whom he may devour (1 Peter 5:8).

Satan's Three Weapons

Satan uses three methods to try to destroy the Christian's faith: First, he tries to make life so miserable that they give up their faith in Christ. The persecution may be physical, social, or mental. Satan will try anything to destroy faith in Christ through persecution.

His second method is to dazzle Christians with the allurements of the world. In 1 Timothy 6:10 Paul warns of this great danger. "For the love of money is a root of all kinds of evil."

Paul is not saying that money is the root of evil but the *love* of money. Many, in their eagerness for money, wander from the faith. If materialism becomes a god, faith in Christ will lose out. "Some have wandered from the faith and pierced themselves with many grief's,"Paul writes in 1 Timothy 6:10. It is not a sin to be rich, but Christians must be aware that the love of money is the root of all evil—for money is the primary ingredient that runs this world. Sinful nature is never satisfied with what it has. It always wants more. And the more it strives, the further it pushes Jesus to the background. Eventually sinful nature pushes Him aside altogether.

The third, and one of the most successful methods the devil has ever used to destroy faith, is by perverting the gospel. He succeeded in Galatia—which is why Paul wrote his letter to the Galatians. Paul tells us in Galatians 5:4 that anyone who tries to add works or law-keeping as a requirement for salvation has fallen from grace. Genuine justification by faith always produces good works, and those good works are always in harmony with God's law. This is true because love (which produces good works) is the fulfillment of the law. When we love others in the same way Christ loves us, we actually fulfill the law because the faith of Jesus produces works that glorify God, in harmony with His law. The fruits of the Spirit are not against the law but in harmony with it (Galatians 5:22, 23).

Christians must be on guard constantly. One of the devil's deceptions is to persuade the believer that once he or she has become a Christian that heaven is automatically theirs. Yes, it is theirs, as long as they believe. But the day they turn their backs on Christ, God can do no more for them. It is not God who rejects them; they are the ones who reject God and tie His hands.

This is why, even though the flesh is against God and is a slave to sin, the believers' hearts must always be focused on Christ, their Savior, their Hope, and their Redemption.

CHAPTER 7
Christ—The True Sabbath Rest
Hebrews 4:1-13

The adult generation of Israelites delivered from Egypt in the Exodus never arrived in Canaan, the Promised Land. We discovered last chapter, in our study of Hebrews 3, why all but two men—Joshua and Caleb—died before they reached their destination.

God kept His promise of deliverance. But because the people hardened their hearts in unbelief they were unable to receive the full benefit of that deliverance. Persistent unbelief is the one sin God cannot forgive. If God were to force all mankind into heaven, then salvation would not be a gift but a requirement. The Bible clearly states that God so loved the world that He gave His only begotten Son that whosoever *believes* (italics mine), should not perish but have everlasting life.

The Promise of Rest

Hebrews 3:19 underscores the importance of belief: "So we see they were not able to enter because of their unbelief." In Hebrews 4, entering Canaan is identified with God's rest—which is then linked to the gospel. This, in turn, is linked to the Sabbath: "Therefore, since the promise of entering his rest still stands, let us be careful that none of you be found to have fallen short of it. For we also have had the gospel preached to us just as they did; but the message they heard was of no value to them, because those who heard did not combine it with faith. Now we who have believed enter that rest, just as God has said, 'So I declared on oath in my anger, They shall never enter my rest. And yet his work has been finished since the creation of the world. For somewhere he has spoken about the seventh day in these words: 'And on the seventh day God rested from all his work'" (Hebrews 4:1-4).

The reality of the Sabbath, as any other truth taught in the Bible, must be linked with the gospel of salvation by grace alone. Otherwise it becomes a legalistic requirement—as it did for the Jews. According to Hebrews 4, faith response to the gospel is symbolized by keeping the Sabbath, which is God's rest. This rest is the gospel—all that God has given the world in Christ. Hence the Sabbath, which is linked with that rest, is vitally linked with justification by faith—the only means of salvation.

Much discussion, unfortunately, surrounds which day is the Sabbath. But before we consider that problem, we need to look at the significance of the Sabbath. After all, it is not the Sabbath day that saves us. It is the truth to which that day points that saves us. Hebrews 4:1-13 clearly reveals the significance of the Sabbath and its connection with the gospel.

Hebrews 3—especially verses 7-19 about the Israelites' Exodus from Egypt to Canaan—tells us that this journey symbolizes the plan of salvation. It was deliverance from Egypt (Egypt symbolizes the world) to Canaan (Canaan symbolizes heaven). In Hebrews 4 the writer uses the failure of the Israelites to enter Canaan as a warning to the Jews of New Testament times. He urges them not to repeat that mistake and be deprived of real rest with Christ in the heavenly Canaan.

With this background, we now read in Hebrews 4:1: "Therefore, since the promise of entering his rest still stands, let us be careful that none of you be found to have fallen short of it."

Just as the majority of the Israelites who left Egypt never made it to Canaan, Paul is suggesting that those who accept the good news of salvation are in danger of losing their faith and being lost.

Canaan was not the real rest; it was a shadow of heaven, which can be reached only in Christ. It is not enough to accept Christ as Savior—to believe in Him as the Messiah. Faith in Him must endure to the end. Paul brings this out again and again in Hebrews, for this is the great danger the Jewish believers of the first century face—just as all Christians do today. The Jews' situation is much worse, however, for they are being persecuted both by fellow Jews who have rejected Christ and by the Gentile world.

In Hebrews 4:2 Paul tells us that both the Israelites of the Exodus and the New Testament Jews have heard the gospel. At the Exodus the Israelites were exposed to the gospel through the Sanctuary model— God's visual aid for the plan of salvation. It was His "Show and Tell."

The New Testament Jews in the first century have heard the gospel through the preaching of Christ—the reality of the Sanctuary model.

Paul tells us that the Jews of the Exodus failed to enter Canaan because their knowledge of the gospel was not accompanied by faith. Hebrews 4: 2 says, "For we also have had the gospel preached to us, just as they did." The "we" refers to the Jews of New Testament times; the "they" refers to Israelites of the Exodus. "But the message they heard was of no value to them, because those who heard did not combine it with faith."

Paul is saying that a knowledge of the gospel is of no value in salvation unless accompanied by faith. As long the believers remain faithful to Jesus Christ, their salvation is guaranteed. But if they harden their hearts through unbelief (as those who died in the wilderness), God makes it clear that He cannot save them, though He very much wants to do so.

Many Christians have misunderstood the wrath of God by equating it with human anger. When the Bible talks of God's wrath, it speaks of it as nearly opposite to human wrath. Human wrath causes loss of rational inhibitions and self control. Human anger explodes. But God's wrath is passive.

Too many Christians are afraid of God because of His "wrath". To understand God better, they should begin by reading Romans 5:8, where God is defined as Love. Love is not just one of His attributes. It is His very nature, His character. Everything about God must be understood in the context of His love. "God is love" (1 John 4:8).

God's Wrath in Romans

With this in mind, Christians must look at God's "wrath" in the context of His love. The Epistle of Romans contains the clearest explanation of the gospel. After its author, Paul, introduces the epistle's theme in Romans 1:15-17, he immediately plunges into the universal sin problem. First Paul says that he is now ready to preach the gospel to those who are in Rome and that he is not ashamed of this gospel because it is the power of God unto salvation, first to the Jew and then to the Gentile. The gospel, he says, is the righteousness of God.

In Romans 1:18, then, he says, "The wrath of God is being revealed from heaven against all ungodliness and wickedness of men who suppress the truth by their wickedness". Notice that Paul is dealing with two basic problems of sinful man. The first is godlessness, or ungodliness.

Ungodliness in this context means deliberately turning one's back on God—living independently of God. Such living results in wickedness, says the apostle.

Many today believe that wickedness is an inherently human problem. But Paul disagrees. Wickedness is the *evidence* of a problem, not the problem *itself.* The problem today is ungodliness. The more people, nations, or communities turn their backs on God, in like measure crime and unrighteousness increase, for these are the fruits of ungodliness. In contrast the fruits of godliness—justification by faith—produce lives in harmony with God's law. Godly lives reveal His love, which seeketh not its own but lives for others.

Though they have the knowledge of God through nature and revelation and their conscience, mankind is deliberately turning its back on God. Romans 1:24 tells us the result: "Therefore, God gave them over to the sinful desires of their hearts, to sexual immorality for the degrading of their bodies with one another."

Continuing in verse 26, Paul says, "Because of this, God gave them over to shameful lusts. Even their women exchanging natural relations for unnatural ones." Verse 27 says the same has happened with men. Verse 28 concludes, "Furthermore, since they did not think it worthy to retain the knowledge of God he gave them over to a depraved mind, to do what ought not to be done."

God says that if men and women choose to live without Him, He has to honor that choice. Hence the terrible world conditions that make our planet a very difficult place on which to live.

Paul in Hebrews 4 tells his readers that if they do not accompany their knowledge of the gospel with a faith response, then they are actually turning their backs on God's supreme Sacrifice, Jesus Christ. If that happens, God will have to let them go, and the consequences of this wrath (a passive letting go) is death. "The wages of sin is death" (Romans 6:23).

Sabbath and Salvation

Hebrews 4:4 links the Sabbath with the plan of salvation, the gospel of Jesus Christ, and mankind's response to it. Paul here also links the Sabbath with justification by faith. To establish context, we must read verse 3: "Now we who have believed enter that rest, just as God has said, 'So I declare on oath in my anger, They shall never enter my rest.'"

Those who deliberately, persistently, and ultimately reject the gift of salvation have chosen death. God does not use compulsion. He does not force salvation on those who reject it. He took the initiative and obtained eternal redemption for all. This is what the last part of verse 3 says: "And yet his work has been finished since the creation of the world."

On the sixth day of creation God (actually Jesus Himself, according to John 1:13) completed His good and perfect creative work. Genesis 2:1 and 2 says: "Thus the heavens and the earth were completed and all their vast array." Verse 3 then says He rested from all His work. He rested, not because He was tired, but because His work was perfect and finished.

Both Old and New Testaments clearly state that the Sabbath does not belong to man. Yes, it was made for man, but it belongs to God. Exodus 20:11 says: "The seventh day is the Sabbath of the Lord thy God."

Exodus 31 brings forward the same idea—that the Sabbath belongs to God. Isaiah 58:13 and 14 calls the Sabbath "Holy of the Lord". In the New Testament Jesus Himself says, "I am the Lord of the Sabbath."

The Sabbath belongs to God because He is the One who did the work. God rested on the Sabbath because His work was perfect and finished. The Sabbath tells us even today that our salvation is guaranteed in Christ. God's Sabbath, incidentally, is our Saturday.

From the creation of the world the plan of salvation was already settled. Ephesians 1:4 tells us that God chose men and women in Christ from the foundation of the world to be holy and blameless. Salvation is a finished work to which mankind has contributed nothing, nor can contribute anything. But without faith, that finished salvation is only an objective (intended) reality and for it to become a subjective (completed) experience in human beings, it must be accompanied by faith. God has created man with a free will, and those who harden their hearts in unbelief can and do reject the gift of salvation in Jesus. This is the thought of Hebrews 4, beginning with verse 4: "For somewhere he has spoken about the Sabbath day in these words: 'And on the Sabbath God rested from all his work (*because His work was perfect and finished*).' And again in the passage above he says, "They shall never enter my rest."

"They" are those who reject the gift of salvation in Christ. They are the unbelievers, those who deliberately turn their backs on God.

Hebrews 4:5 and 6 says: "It still remains that some still enter that rest, and those who formerly had the gospel preached to them did not go in, because of their disobedience." Notice that the gospel was preached to the Israelites of the Exodus through the Sanctuary service. They did not enter the Promised Land—a type or antecedent of heaven—because of disobedience (to the gospel, not to the law). Verse 7 says, "Therefore, God again set a certain day, calling it Today, when a long time later he spoke through David as was said before: 'Today, if you hear his voice, do not harden your hearts.'"

Paul is saying, "Do not reject God's wonderful gift of salvation in Christ." Then, quoting verse 8, he writes, "For if Joshua had given them rest, God would not have spoken later about another day."

We need to understand the phrase, "another day." The Joshua of Exodus brought them into Canaan, but Canaan was not the real rest. It was a *type* of the real rest. The real rest is in Jesus Christ. "Another day" refers to the coming of Christ who, by His perfect life and sacrificial death, brought the real rest that by faith all believers can enjoy.

Verse 9 continues: "There remains, then, a Sabbath-rest for the people of God." The book of Hebrews was written to the Jews; therefore the phrase "people of God" does not refer to Christians but to the Jewish nation that still calls itself the people of God. These Jews were keeping the Sabbath then and to this day keep the Sabbath. They are indeed keeping the right day, but Paul is saying that it is not the day that saves. It is the *significance* of the day. Keeping the day has no value without Jesus, the Lord of that day. The Jews are keeping the day, but they have no true rest.

When Jesus began His earthly ministry to Jews who were struggling to make it to heaven by the works of the law, He said, "Come unto Me, all you that labor (*who are desperately trying to make it to heaven by your own performance*) and I will give you rest" (Matthew 11:28). The Sabbath rest points to Jesus Christ, who through His perfect life and sacrificial death obtained eternal redemption for mankind. Jesus cried on the cross, "It is finished." At the end of creation, the sixth day of the week, the heavens and the earth were finished; so also on the cross, the sixth day of the week (Friday), redemption (begun before the foundation of the world) was at last finished. By His perfect life Jesus met the positive demands of the law. By His sacrificial death He met the justice of the law. He changed the status of mankind from condemnation to justification. This was accomplished on Friday, the sixth day of the week. He then rested in the tomb on the Sabbath. The resurrection on Sunday did not add to the righteousness of Christ that saved us, but confirmed it (Romans 1:4; 4:25).

This is the supreme gift God offers. Those who have accepted that gift now must hold onto their faith in Christ.

God's Supreme Gift

Verse 10 continues, "For anyone who enters God's rest also rests from his own work, just as God did from his." Those who enter God's rest will stop trying to add their works as a contribution to their justification. Genuine justification *does* produce works, but those works are the fruit of salvation. They do not contribute one iota toward justification. Justification is entirely a free gift from God. Paul says in Romans 3:24, "Being justified freely by the redemption (*or through the redemption that is in Christ Jesus)*".

Since salvation is a gift, therefore, those who enter into God's rest will stop trying to save themselves. Otherwise, Paul warns in Galatians 5:4, they will surely fall from grace altogether.

Paul concludes his thought in Hebrews 4:11 with these words: "Let us, therefore, make every effort to enter that rest, so that no one will fall by following their example of disobedience." Whatever the situation, believers must never give up their faith, though it may mean persecution, ridicule, or hardship in this world. Christians are living in enemy territory, but their citizenship is in heaven as long as their faith is in Christ.

God who reads mankind's thoughts makes a distinction between actions and motives. Anything we do that is not faith-motivated is sin, (Romans 14:23) for in His eyes eating and drinking and even keeping of the Sabbath can be sin. Paul continues in verses 12 and 13, "For the word of God is living and active. Sharper than any double-edged sword, it penetrates even to dividing soul and spirit, joints and marrow; it judges the thoughts and attitudes of the heart. Nothing in all creation is hidden from God's sight. Everything is uncovered and laid bare before the eyes of him to whom we must give account."

God looks at the heart. He knows that human beings struggle in this world and sometimes fall. But the big question remains, "Where is your heart?" Is it resting in the righteousness of Christ? Paul says in 1 Corinthians 4:5 that when mankind stands before the judgment seat of Christ, our very thoughts will be brought up, for God is more concerned with motivation than mere acts.

The Pharisees expertly and zealously kept the letter of the law God had given them. Yet Jesus told them in so many words, "You are very particular about paying your tithe, even regarding the cumin and mint you grow. But you lack the weightier matters of the law which is love" (See Matthew 23:23).

It is my prayer that all who read this book will not only believe in Jesus Christ, the Source of salvation, but that this faith will endure unto the end. May the Sabbath be kept for the right reason—not to earn salvation, but because it is a sign between God and His people that they have entered into His rest. This is why God gave the Sabbath, right from the very beginning of creation. While God gave Adam and Eve complete dominion over this world, God made it clear they had to be God-dependent. The Sabbath was a sign of that dependence.

Adam's and Eve's very first day on this earth was not spent doing things but resting in God's finished creation. Only after they turned their backs on God did He tell them, basically, "From now on you shall eat your food by the sweat of your brow" (See Genesis 3:19).

Those who are resting in Christ for their salvation and for whom the Sabbath has become a sign of righteousness know they are heaven bound, for God has promised. But if they turn their backs on God, they will then have to earn their own way to salvation. The Bible says that by the works of the law no flesh will be justified. The only hope for salvation comes from holding onto faith in Christ.

CHAPTER 8

Christ—Our High Priest
Hebrews 4:14–5:10

We covered Hebrews 4: 1-13 in our last study, where Paul, the writer of Hebrews, points to the Sabbath as a day of rest, set aside for mankind as a constant reminder of God's perfect and finished work for the human race. The Sabbath, we learned, is a reminder both of creation and redemption, with true redemptive significance when seen in light of the gospel. It also reminds us of the future restoration (Isaiah 66:22).

Now in Hebrews 4:14-8:6 and beyond, Paul turns his attention to Christ as the believers' great and merciful High Priest in the heavenly Sanctuary.

To benefit fully from this study as God reveals it in Scripture, we will first read Hebrews 4:14—5:1-10 and then study it in detail: "Therefore, since we have a great high priest who has gone through the heavens, Jesus the Son of God, let us hold firmly to the faith we profess. For we do not have a high priest who is unable to sympathize with our weaknesses, but we have one who has been tempted in every way, just as we are—yet was without sin. Let us then approach the throne of grace with confidence, so that we may receive mercy and find grace to help us in our time of need. Every high priest is selected from among men and is appointed to represent them in matters related to God, to offer gifts and sacrifices for sins. He is able to deal gently with those who are ignorant and are going astray, since he himself is subject to weakness. This is why he has to offer sacrifices for his own sins, as well as for the sins of the people. No one takes this honor upon himself; he must be called by God, just as Aaron was. So Christ also did not take upon himself the glory of becoming a high priest. But God said to him, "You are my Son; today I have become your Father." And He says in another place, "You are a priest forever, in the order of Melchizedek." During the days of Jesus' life on earth, he offered up prayers and petitions with loud cries and tears to the one who could save him from death, and he was heard because of his reverent submission. Although he was a son, he learned obedience from what he suffered and, once made perfect, he became the source of eternal salvation for all who obey him and was designated by God to be high priest in the order of Melchizedek."

Why This Priestly Ministry?

Why is so much emphasis given here to Christ's priestly ministry? First, we must remember that the Epistle to the Hebrews was written with Jewish believers in mind. These believers are very discouraged because of intense pressure coming at them from every direction. They need to be fully established in Christ so their faith can be unshakeable built on the Rock, Jesus Christ, who saved them through His earthly mission and now sits at the right hand of God, interceding for them and representing them against the accusations of Satan. Furthermore, their faith needed to be established in view of the coming destruction which took place in 70 A.D.

The word "priest" means one who represents the congregation before God. It means the opposite of "prophet." A prophet *represents God before the people;* but a priest *represents the people before God.* Having fully and completely redeemed humanity, Jesus took a perfect, redeemed human nature in Himself to heaven to represent mankind as its Substitute. Christ, as the believers' Priest, mediates on behalf of all Christians on earth who struggle because they are still sinners.

Paul states the case succinctly in Hebrews 8:1 and 2: "We do have such a high priest, who sat down at the right hand of the throne of the Majesty in heaven, and who serves in the sanctuary, the true tabernacle set up by the Lord, and not by man."

Assurance of salvation is not only validated by what Christ did during His earthly mission. We must also look at Christ as a High Priest who defends, intercedes, and who will vindicate His followers in the judgment because they trust in Him.

Because Christians live in enemy territory, their lives will always be a struggle spiritually, socially, economically, and even physically. For this reason they need a Priest who has gone through those same situations Himself and can sympathize with them and help them in their struggles. In Christ they have just such a Priest! This is the whole point of Hebrews 4:14-16: "Therefore, since we have a great high priest who has gone through the heavens, Jesus the Son of God, let us hold firmly to the faith we profess. For we do not have a high priest who is unable to sympathize with our weaknesses, but we have one who has been tempted in every way, just as we are—yet was without sin. Let us then approach the throne of grace with confidence, so that we may receive mercy and find grace to help us in our time of need."

Remember what we are told in Hebrews 2:17 and 18—that just as human beings are made of flesh and blood, Jesus assumed the very same nature. He became One with humanity, for only in this way could He legally be its Savior and later its High Priest. A priest must represent the people to whom he belongs, so He must be made in all points "like unto us" so that He can be a faithful Savior and a merciful High Priest.

Jesus in Heaven

After satisfying the law in every respect and obtaining salvation full and complete for the human race by His perfect life and sacrificial death, Jesus returned to heaven to intercede on behalf of all those who have accepted His righteousness by faith.

According to what we just read in Hebrews 4:15,16, Christ as High Priest understands human weakness and struggles against temptation. The verse is not referring primarily to physical weakness but to spiritual weakness. Jesus assumed the very same humanity to which we belong. He was of the seed of David and of Abraham. He became one of us and struggled as we do. But while all humans fail and fall and sin, Christ never sinned. Not even by a thought did He yield to the temptations that came to Him. Now He presents His victorious life to the Father on mankind's behalf.

In view of these facts, Christians can come with full confidence to the throne of grace and obtain two things: (1) Mercy, because of their failures, and (2) Grace, or help, in the time of need.

The word grace is used in two ways in the New Testament. Primarily it means God's loving disposition toward humanity in which He redeemed sinners through the gift of Jesus Christ in His earthly mission.

But in 1 Corinthians 15:9 and 10, 2 Corinthians 12:7-10, and Philippians 4:13, we discover that grace can also refer to the strength—that is, the power of God—made available to believers who are standing under the umbrella of justification by faith.

In 2 Corinthians 12:7-10 Paul talks about a thorn in his flesh from Satan that God allows to help keep Paul humble. Paul had prayed earnestly three times asking God to remove it. God's answer was, "My grace is sufficient for you, for my strength is made perfect in weakness." Paul then responded, "I will gladly rejoice in my weakness that the power of God, (*which is grace*) may rest upon me."

Not only does mankind therefore have a merciful High Priest who can sympathize with its weakness and struggles, but this Priest can help in struggles against the flesh, temptation, and sin.

Four Priestly Qualifications

We now turn to Hebrews 5, where Paul deals with the qualifications—the full prerequisites—required of a priest. After describing the four requirements, Paul points out that Christ met all four of them.

In Hebrews 5:1 we find the first requirement. "Every high priest is selected from among men and is appointed to represent them in matters related to God, to offer gifts and sacrifices for sin."

A priest has to be chosen from among those he represents. To represent mankind before God, Christ had to become a man. Hebrews 5:7-9 says that He was in all points a human being. Though He was indeed the Son of God, He became one of us. He suffered and was made perfect through suffering and went to heaven to represent us.

The second requirement, according to Hebrews 5:3, is that a priest be able to offer gifts and sacrifices. Earthly priests offered animals and other gifts from the people, but the spotless lambs they sacrificed and the blood they took into the Sanctuary was not able to redeem mankind—for the simple reason that these gifts were only a type, or shadow, of Jesus Christ.

Christ now offers to God only one gift and only one sacrifice—His righteousness, perfect in every way—for us. Through that gift He is able to save us to the uttermost.

Romans 5:18 confirms that this gift is indeed the righteousness of Christ, given to us at His death on the cross. His life—lived out on this earth for 33 years—fully satisfied the positive demands of the law. This is God's gift to us. And through His death He satisfied the justice of the law, for the law offers only two options—obey and live; disobey and die. All mankind has unfortunately disobeyed the law. So to meet both the requirements, Jesus had to live a perfect life as our Substitute and then meet the justice of the law through the cross to cancel our sins. His doing and His dying is the gift and the sacrifice that He presents before God on behalf of all those who believe.

"My dear children, I write this (*the good news of salvation*) to you so that you will not sin," the Apostle John records in 1 John 2:1. "Sin" here appears in the plural. The gospel cannot condone sinning, for this good news saves mankind not only from sin's guilt and punishment but also from its slavery and power.

Romans 6:22 and 23 brings this out very clearly: "Having been set free from sin, and having become slaves of God, you have your fruit to holiness, and the end, everlasting life" (NKJV).

The Apostle John notes, however, that sinful natures do indeed struggle and sometimes fall short. So he adds in 1 John 2:1, second half: "But if anybody does sin, we have one who speaks to the Father in our defense—Jesus Christ, the Righteous One. He is the atoning sacrifice for our sins, and not only for ours but also for the sins of the whole world." Jesus offers His righteousness and His blood—His sacrifice—on behalf of the human race.

The third requirement for a priest, says Paul, is that he must have personally struggled with weak, sinful flesh and be able to sympathize with the weak, sinful human beings he represents. Hebrews 5:2 says: "He is able to deal gently with those who are ignorant and are going astray, since he himself is subject to weakness."

We must never say or teach that Christ had a sinful nature. Human beings have a sinful nature. What Jesus did was to assume a humanity that was not His by nature—a human nature in need of redeeming. The Bible says Jesus was made flesh—made of a woman. He was made under the law, says Galatians 4:4 and 5. He was made sin (See 2 Corinthians 5:21). He was made what He was not by native right, for by right He was divine. But because He had to qualify as our Savior, God joined that divinity of His Son to our humanity in the womb of Mary. In doing so, Christ became qualified to be Savior and High Priest for humanity.

During His 33 years on this earth, He knew what it meant to struggle against the flesh. He knew what it meant to deny the flesh. Jesus tells us in Luke 9:23, "If anyone would come after me, he must deny himself and take up his cross daily and follow me." Christ bore the wooden cross for only a few hours, but the principle of the cross— self-denial—He carried all His life. His constant attitude was, "Not My will, but the will of My Father. I came, not to do My will, but the will of My Father. Not I, but My Father" (See John 5:30).

Humanity's High Priest truly was chosen from among humanity. Jesus can offer perfect gifts and a perfect sacrifice. He understands human weaknesses and struggles, for He, Himself experienced them all while on earth.

The fourth and final requirement of a priest is that he cannot be self-appointed—he must be chosen by God, as Aaron was. Hebrews 5:4 says, "No one takes this honor upon himself; he must be called by God just as Aaron was."

The Jews were already familiar with these four priestly requirements from their reading of the Old Testament, so Paul presses forward, pointing out in Hebrews 5:5-10 that Jesus Christ meets all of them: "So Christ also did not take upon himself the glory of becoming a high priest but God said to him, 'You are my Son; today I have become your Father.' And he says in another place, 'You are a priest forever in the order of Melchizedek.'" Christ could not be a Priest according to the order of Levi, for He was born of the tribe of Judah. Later in our study we will discover the significant differences between the Levitical priesthood and the Melchizedek priesthood. What we are told in Hebrews 5:1-10 is that Christ was chosen by God to be mankind's High Priest and that He met the fourth requirement, covered in Hebrews 5:1-4.

An Intercessory Life

In Hebrews 5:7 Paul continues telling us about Christ's experience: "During the days of Jesus' life on earth, he offered up prayers and petitions with loud cries and tears to the one who could save him from death, and he was heard because of his reverent submission."

Notice that here the word "days" is in the plural. This means the writer is referring not only to Christ in Gethsemane but to His entire experience on earth. Jesus' continual prayer seems to have been, "Not I, but you, Father, must live through Me. Not I, but You must conquer this flesh. Not I, but You must give Me the power to endure the cross."

Throughout His earthly life Jesus struggled, but He was made perfect through His suffering in that struggle. Verse 8 tells us, "Although he was a son, he learned obedience from what he suffered and, once made perfect, he became the source of eternal salvation for all who obey him."

The word translated "obey" here is the same as the word for faith. Faith is more than a simple mental assent to truth. It is the surrender of the will to the truth as it is in Christ. Faith is saying, "I am crucified with

Christ, but I am still living. It is not I, but Christ lives in me. And the life I now live, I live by faith in the Son of God who loved me and gave Himself for me" (Galatians 2:20).

We conclude with Hebrews 5:9,10: "And, once made perfect, he became the source of eternal salvation for all who obey him and was designated by God to be high priest in the order of Melchizedek." To know Christ as only a Savior is not enough. He must also be known as High Priest—for three reasons.

Importance of Christ's Priesthood

Martin Luther provides the first reason Christ should be recognized for His priesthood: All believers are sinners and righteous simultaneously— sinners in themselves and righteous in Him. As long as they are sinners, they need a Mediator—a go-between with a Holy God.

The second reason is that weak sinners especially need a Priest who can sympathize with their weakness. And third, believers need Someone who is able to help them in their weakness and struggles against temptation and sinful flesh.

It is now clear that in Christ the believers possess a High Priest who is able to sympathize with their weakness—One who is able to help them in their needs and can forgive them and have mercy when they fail. They can truly praise God for such a perfect Savior and merciful, sympathetic High Priest who is able to save them to the uttermost.

Salvation is entirely a gift from God. Other than giving their heartfelt assent to salvation through faith, Christian believers can do nothing to advance their salvation.

Jesus first obtained salvation by His life and death in His earthly mission. Now as a perfect Savior He represents mankind, with every vestige of sin destroyed at the cross. When Jesus rose from the dead, nothing that belonged to sin rose with Him. He left sin in the grave. He left condemned humanity in the grave. He rose with a glorified humanity, completely cleansed from sin.

By the time Jesus arrived on earth, the Jews had thoroughly perverted the Sanctuary message. When Jesus saw the moneychangers exploiting the people in the temple, He became righteously indignant and chased the merchants out, crying, "How dare you turn the house of God into a den of thieves?" (See Matthew 21:13 and Luke 19:46). The cleansing of the temple illustrates the cleansing of humanity. The Bible—especially the New Testament—refers to the believer's body as a temple of God. Paul says in 1 Corinthians 3:16, "Don't you know that you yourselves are God's temple and that God's spirit lives in you?"

This temple which has been ruined and corrupted by the fall into sin has been cleansed in Jesus Christ. Paul says in Philippians 3:20 and 21 that the Christian's citizenship is now in heaven, while he or she awaits the coming of the Lord to change the vile body of sin and restore it as a glorious body, already prepared and awaiting His Second Coming.

Their faith must be in a Savior who has already redeemed them and in a High Priest who is interceding for them. Jesus is doing everything He can to save us. Not only has He satisfied all the demands of the law on behalf of humanity, but he now defends His followers, interceding for them in the presence of the Father against the devil, who accuses the brethren day and night.

With Christ as both Savior and High Priest, His followers can be absolutely certain of salvation—but only so long as they remain under the umbrella of justification by faith.

I pray that as we face the ups and downs of life, no matter what we go through, that we will remember that the most valuable thing we possess in this world has nothing to do with material things, employment, pension, or social security. It is faith in Christ. That faith must endure unto the end. We should never give it up.

And when Christ comes, He will say, "Come, inherit the kingdom prepared for you from the foundation of the world." It is my prayer that you who read this book will be part of that great throng around the throne of Jesus Christ after He comes the second time to take home His followers.

Jesus says, "You will know the truth and the truth will set you free" (John 8:32). The truth is Jesus Christ, His birth, His life, His death, His resurrection—that is, the gospel—and Jesus Christ as humanity's High Priest.

Jesus' reassures us, "I am with you till the end of the world" (Matthew 28:20).

CHAPTER 9

The Cost of Abandoning Christ
Hebrews 5:11—6:1-12

This study of Hebrews 5:11 to Hebrews 6:1-12 is vital for those living in the last days. Christians today face a time of trouble such as has never been experienced by any past generation. The message of the Epistle to the Hebrews alternates between encouragement and warning—a fact easily appreciated by reading the entire book in a single sitting.

The book was written to Jewish Christians of New Testament times who were in danger of giving up their faith in Christ and reverting to Judaism.

Last chapter we studied Hebrews 4:14 - 5:1-10, which presents Christ as the believers' faithful and merciful great High Priest. As in the section of Hebrews that presents Christ as Savior, tremendous encouragement comes from discovering that Christ is the believers' High Priest.

Not only can a Christian have salvation full and complete in Christ, he or she can be certain that Christ is seated at the right hand of God to intercede against the accusations of Satan. As High Priest, Christ also shows infinite mercy toward struggling Christians and provides help in time of need. Salvation is truly complete in Jesus Christ.

A Time for Warning

Having encouraged us with a picture of Jesus as High Priest in heaven, Paul in Hebrews 5:11 through 6:12 changes tone to warn his readers of the cost of abandoning their faith in Christ—a warning we do well to heed today. We begin by reading the passage in its entirety, before examining its implications in detail. "We have much to say about this, but it is hard to explain because you are slow to learn. In fact, though by this time you ought to be teachers, you need someone to teach you the elementary truths of God's Word all over again. You need milk, not solid food! Anyone who lives on milk, being still an infant, is not acquainted with the teaching about righteousness. But solid food is for the mature, who by constant use have trained themselves to distinguish good from evil. Therefore let us leave the elementary teachings about Christ and go on to maturity, not laying again that foundation of repentance from acts that lead to death, and of faith in God, instruction about baptisms, the laying on of hands, the resurrection of the dead, and eternal judgment. And God permitting, we will do so. It is impossible for those who have once been enlightened, who have tasted the heavenly gift, who have shared in the Holy Spirit, who have tasted the goodness of the word of God and the powers of the coming age, if they fall away, to be brought back to repentance, because to their loss they are crucifying the Son of God all over again and subjecting him to public disgrace. Land that drinks in the rain often falling on it and that produces a crop useful to those for whom it is farmed receives the blessing of God. But land that produces thorns and thistles is worthless and is in danger of being cursed. In the end it will be burned. Even though we speak like this, dear friends, we are confident of better things in your case—things that accompany salvation. God is not unjust; he will not forget your work and love that you have shown him as you have helped his people and continue to help them. We want each of you to show this same diligence to the very end, in order to make your hope sure. We do not want you to become lazy, but to imitate those who through faith and patience inherit what has been promised."

Two Problems

The passage has two parts. In the first, Hebrews 5:11 to Hebrews 6: 6, Paul deals with the problems and dangers of being babies in Christ. The second part, Hebrews 6:7-12, points out that Christian growth to maturity is essential for ultimate salvation.

With this in mind, let us study the passage in detail. First, we look at the problem of being babies in Christ. Paul has already identified Christ's priestly ministry in the order of the ceaseless ministry of Melchizidek (Hebrews 5:10). Now he immediately introduces a problem in the Christian experience of the Jewish Christians of his day—the problem of spiritual immaturity.

He observes two things: First, immature Christians are incapable of understanding and absorbing the deeper truths revealed in the Word of God. In Hebrews 5:11 he laments, "We have much to say about this (*Christ's ministry in the heavenly Sanctuary*), but it is hard to explain because you are slow to learn."

His second point is equally dismal: Unlike physical growth, Paul says, it takes more than the passage of time to produce spiritual maturity (Hebrews 5:12-14). Young human beings grow physically—nature demands it. Growth may be stunted if they are not well fed and cared for, but they still grow. But Paul is saying that spiritually immature Christians may become stagnant for years without growing at all in grace, in truth, and in knowledge.

These Jewish Christians, says Paul, evidently are not able to absorb or understand the deeper things of God or distinguish between truth and error. Hebrews 5:12-14 says: "In fact, though by this time you ought to be teachers, you need someone to teach you the elementary truths of God's Word all over again. You need milk, not solid food. Anyone who lives on milk, being still an infant, is not acquainted with the teaching about righteousness. But solid food is for the mature, who by constant use have trained themselves to distinguish good from evil."

We all face this problem, especially as life becomes more hectic with our work and other time-absorbing matters. Then we stop taking time to study the Word of God and help one another along the Christian walk. Our spiritual growth stops and we remain babes in Christ. This danger faced the Jewish Christians of Paul's day and it faces us today. It's the same problem that faced the believers at Corinth.

Paul himself had raised up the Corinthian church. Then, about 10 years later, he feels compelled to write his first epistle to them. One reason he writes is out of concern that they have remained babes in Christ. The Christian Corinthians are still unable to absorb solid food from the Word of God, Paul writes in 1 Corinthians 3:1-3. He says: "Brothers, I could not address you as spiritual but as worldly—mere infants in Christ. I gave you milk, not solid food, for you were not yet ready for it. Indeed, you are still not ready. You are still worldly. For since there is jealously and quarreling among you, are you not worldly? Are you not acting like mere men?"

By now the Corinthians should have grown enough spiritually to be able to receive solid, gospel food. When Paul first came to them, 10 years before, they were babes in Christ and could not understand the heavy, deep things of the Word of God. The problem is that they are still babies, 10 years later.

Imagine having a 10-year-old child who still wears diapers and drinks only milk. Christians need to grow in grace and truth, for though they are citizens of heaven and their salvation is guaranteed, they still are living in enemy territory—on dangerous ground.

Immature Christians are indeed at extreme risk, Paul says. They are exceedingly vulnerable to the devil who can so easily pull them out of Christ and manipulate them into becoming enemies of the gospel. Remaining immature Christians can be very costly.

This is brought out in Hebrews 6:1-6: "Therefore let us leave the elementary teachings about Christ and go on to maturity, not laying again the foundation of repentance from acts that lead to death, and of faith in God, instruction about baptisms, the laying on of hands, the resurrection of the dead, the eternal judgment. And God permitting, God will do so."

Paul is listing the things they had first learned about the gospel. They had indeed learned these things, but because they were not maturing in their Christian walk, they had to keep hearing these things over and over again—a tragedy.

But an even greater tragedy is found in Hebrews 6:4-6: "It is impossible for those who have once been enlightened (*Christians who have understood the gospel*) who have tasted the heavenly gift (*born-again Christians who received the gift of the Holy Spirit*), who have shared in the Holy Spirit, who have tasted the goodness of the Word of God (*rejoiced in their salvation in Christ*) and the powers of the coming age."

The "coming age" refers to Christ's Second Coming. Paul in Philippians 3:20 and 21 says Christians are citizens of heaven, looking forward to His coming when He will change their vile bodies into the glorious bodies that He has prepared for them in His earthly mission.

This passage, Hebrews 6:4-6, also is talking about believers—born-again Christians. We cannot escape this reality, and verse 6 says that if these born-again Christians fall away, turn their backs on the gospel, and drive away the Holy Spirit by their persistent resistance to His pleading, they cannot be brought back to repentance, for they are crucifying the Son of God all over again and subjecting Him to public disgrace.

At Enmity with God

Human nature is always at enmity with God. Paul shows this clearly in Romans 8:7. It was this carnal, sinful human nature that truly crucified

Christ. The Jews alone did not crucify Him—it was human nature that turned its back on God. Stephen, the first martyr of the Christian church, in his very first sermon (one that cost him his life) flatly tells the Jewish leaders: "You stiff-necked people, ever since our fathers, you have rejected the truth."

Paul is warning here in Hebrews that those who deliberately, persistently resist the pleading, guidance, and direction of the Holy Spirit and refuse to grow in spirit—in truth, in grace, in knowledge—are in danger of falling away. Falling away means turning their backs to the gospel and Jesus Christ, God, and the promise of salvation.

Those who do this are in danger of losing salvation altogether, Paul says. For it is extremely difficult—in fact, Paul says it is impossible—to be brought back to repentance, because they have crucified the Son of God all over again. Remember, the flesh is at enmity with God. It was the sinful flesh of mankind that crucified Christ. So, there are two ways to look at the cross—two ways to relate to the cross of Christ. Either we cry, "Crucify Him", which is the cry of everyone who has not yet accepted Jesus Christ and is still controlled by the flesh, or we can be crucified *with* Christ. This is the other alternative.

What Paul says about himself in Galatians 2:20 really refers to all believers: "I am crucified with Christ, but I am still living; it is not I but Christ lives in me."

This is the confession of every believer who has accepted Jesus Christ—who has identified with Jesus Christ and Him crucified.

Paul says the same thing in Galatians 6:14, "But God forbid that I should glory except in the cross of our Lord Jesus Christ, by whom the world has been crucified to me (*the lust of the flesh, the lust of the eyes and the pride of life*), and I to the world" (NKJV).

Between the two kingdoms—the church, which is the kingdom of heaven on earth under the banner of Christ, and the world, which is under Satan—stands the cross of Christ. The world cries out, "Crucify Him." The church proclaims, "We have been crucified with Christ." These are the two options in responding to the cross of Christ.

Those who accept Jesus recognize the infinite cost He paid for them. They realize what it cost Him—God-abandonment and the terrible agony of experiencing the wages of sin. Knowing this, how can they possibly turn their backs on Him? How can they knowingly crucify Him again?

On the cross, Jesus cried, "Father, forgive them for they do not know what they are doing." God was willing to forgive those who in ignorance cried out 2,000 years ago, "Crucify Him."

But after the resurrection, these people had no excuse. Caiphas and those who rejected Jesus now had undeniable proof that Jesus was the Messiah.

The Curse Removed

In those days, being crucified was equivalent to being hung on a tree. In Galatians 3:13 Paul says that Christ delivered humanity from the curse of the law, having been made a curse for us. Then Paul quotes from Deuteronomy, the book of the law: "Cursed is everyone who is hung on a tree" (Deuteronomy 21:22).

To apply this word "curse" to a person means to rule out the hope of their resurrection. It means good-bye to life forever. The fact that Jesus broke through this curse and rose from the dead was the greatest proof that He was the Messiah.

Those who understand this and still deliberately turn their backs on Christ are no longer crucifying Him out of ignorance. They are deliberately, knowingly crying out "Crucify Him." How can they do this and once again experience repentance?

Verses 4-6 do not apply to discouraged Christians who for one reason or another have stopped going to church. These are still believers. They may be extremely weak Christians—carnal Christians, babes in Christ on dangerous ground. But as long as they believe in Christ, their salvation is sure. These non-attending Christians have not yet committed the unpardonable sin, but they are in danger of doing so.

Addressing the Jewish believers who are babies in Christ in danger of losing their salvation in Hebrews 10:25, Paul says, "Do not forsake the assembling of the brethren." In other words, "Do not stop going to church, because we need each other to grow in grace and truth."

Essential Christian Growth

Christian growth is essential. In the second part of his warning message, Paul reminds his readers that those who cultivate His grace and cooperate with God will find great blessings because ultimately their faith will become unshakeable.

Those who fail to nurture their Christian experience by feeding their spiritual nature, on the other hand, will be disappointed and lose their salvation. Hebrews 6:7 says: "Land that drinks in the rain often falling on it and that produces a crop useful to those for whom it is farmed receives the blessing of God." When a farmer cultivates his land and makes sure the weeds are destroyed, plows it and plants the seed, he receives the blessing of what he has sown. On the other hand, verse 8 says that neglected land produces thorns and thistles that are worth nothing but to be burned. Paul says in verse 9 that Christians must be warned to spend time with the Word of God and grow in grace and truth—that is, to grow spiritually. Past spiritual experiences are not enough. Faith in Christ must be continually cultivated and strengthened through Bible study, witnessing, and involvement in Christian service until it reaches a state where it can endure unto the end.

Paul, the Farmer

In our final passage for this chapter, we read in Hebrews 6:9-12: "Even though we speak like this, dear friends (*even though I am using this illustration of the land*) we are confident of better things in your case."

Paul is saying that he trusts that his readers will be like the farmer who cultivates his land. Study and spiritual growth accompany salvation. God is not unjust. He will not forget the work and love Christians invest in helping their brothers and sisters grow. Therefore, Christians should not forsake their gatherings in church. For it is here that they can help each other grow spiritually. The church is the body of Christ, and just as all parts of the human body need one another—the hands need the legs, the ears need the eyes—so Christians need one another as the body of Christ.

In verse 12 Paul says, "We do not want you to become lazy, but to imitate those who through faith and patience inherit what has been promised." Nowhere in Scripture do we find "Once saved, always saved." While it is true that as long as Christians hold onto their faith, they have full assurance of salvation. But while they are citizens of heaven, they are still living in enemy territory. The righteousness that entitles them to heaven now and in the judgment is in Christ. No one can touch this righteousness, because Christ is in heaven and His righteousness is indestructible. No thief can steal it from Him.

But the faith that makes that righteousness transferable to the Christian is vulnerable, for it resides in them. Satan has access to this faith—he can touch it. His ultimate goal is to do so through persecution, perversion of the gospel, or by enticing the Christian by dangling before them the trinkets of the world.

Jesus essentially tells His disciples in Matthew 10:17-22, "Your faith must endure unto the end and only such people will be saved." Christians will be persecuted and brought before councils, but they must not give up their faith.

Paul summarizes this beautifully in Hebrews 10:35-39: "Therefore do not cast away your confidence; which has great reward. For you have need of endurance, so that after you have done the will of God (*held onto your faith to the end*) you will receive the promise: 'For yet a little while, And He who is coming will come and will not tarry.' Now the just shall live by faith; But if anyone draws back. My soul has no pleasure in him (*if you say good-bye to your faith*). But we are not of those who draw back to perdition, but of those who believe to the saving of the soul" (NKJV).

May God bless us that we may be among those who are represented in Hebrews 10:39.

CHAPTER 10

The Certainty of God's Promises
Hebrews 6:13-20

In the first half of Hebrews 6 (which we studied last chapter), Paul reveals a sobering and dangerous possibility—that Christians may decide to turn their backs on Christ in unbelief and lose their salvation altogether. It is of utmost importance, Paul says, that Christians grow in their spiritual experience so their faith becomes unshakeable, no matter what happens to them. This is, in fact, one of the main points of the Epistle to the Hebrews.

In the second half of Hebrews 6 (verses 13 to 20), Paul changes tactics from warning to encouragement. He uses the experience of Abraham, the father of the Jewish nation, as an example of how one must never give up faith in God's promises.

We begin this study, as usual, by reading the passage (Hebrews 6:13-20) in its entirety and then analyzing each phrase: "When God made his promise to Abraham, since there was no one greater for him to swear by, he swore by himself, saying, 'I will surely bless you and give you many descendants.' And so after waiting patiently, Abraham received what was promised. Men swear by someone greater than themselves, and the oath confirms what is said and puts an end to all argument. Because God wanted to make the unchanging nature of his purpose very clear to the heirs of what was promised, he confirmed it with an oath. God did this so that, by two unchangeable things in which it is impossible for God to lie, we who have fled to take hold of the hope offered to us may be greatly encouraged. We have this hope as an anchor for the soul, firm and secure. It enters the inner sanctuary behind the curtain, where Jesus, who went before us, has entered on our behalf. He has become a high priest forever, in the order of Melchizedek."

Blessing to the Gentiles

In verses 13 and 14 Paul tells us that God came to Abraham with a promise, backed—or guaranteed—by an oath. The original promise to Abraham is recorded in Genesis 22:17 and 18 and contains a wonderful blessing for non-Jews: "I will surely bless you and make your descendants as numerous as the stars in the sky and as the sand on the seashore. Your descendants will take possession of the cities of their enemies, and through your offspring all nations on earth will be blessed, because you have obeyed me."

At the very heart of this promise are the words "Through your offspring or seed." Abraham is being told that all nations of the earth will be blessed. The initial promise given to Abraham pertained to his son, Isaac, but when we read verse 18, we notice the word "offspring" or seed is in the singular. The immediate seed, or offspring, of Abraham was Isaac. But Isaac is apparently not the blessing promised to the whole human race. God has another plan whereby a later descendant will fulfill that blessing.

In his Epistle to the Galatian Christians, Paul clearly shows that the ultimate seed—the descendant through whom all the nations would be blessed—is none other than Jesus Christ, the Savior of the world.

Paul writes in Galatians 3:16: "The promises were spoken to Abraham and to his seed. The Scripture does not say 'and to seeds' meaning many people, but 'and to your seed,' meaning one person, who is Christ." Christ's humanity was the corporate humanity of the entire race, enabling God through Jesus to offer redemption to all. This by no means suggests that the entire human race will go to heaven. Unfortunately, many will be lost, not because God has not kept His promise, but because they deliberately and ultimately reject the salvation accomplished in Christ.

It is faith in this promised Seed—Christ—that kept Abraham faithful to God unto the very end. Christ said this to the Jews of His day about Abraham's faith: "Your father Abraham rejoiced at the thought of seeing my day; he saw it (by faith) and was glad" (John 8:56).

Likewise, believers by faith today must see in Jesus their ultimate salvation. They must hold onto that faith until the very end. They must grow and mature as Christians so that their faith may become unshakeable. This is the whole point of Hebrews. That same enduring faith of Abraham is shared by all the Old Testament giants listed in Hebrews 11.

Hebrews 11:32-40 tells us plainly the kind of faith Paul believes Christians should have: "And what more shall I say? I do not have time to tell about Gideon, Barak, Samson, Jephthah, David, Samuel and the prophets, who through faith conquered kingdoms, administered justice, and gained what was promised; who shut the mouths of lions, quenched the fury of the flames, and escaped the edge of the sword; whose weakness was turned to strength; and who became powerful in battle and routed foreign armies. Women received back their dead, raised to life again. Others were tortured and refused to be released, so that they might gain a better resurrection. Some faced jeers and flogging, while still others were chained and put in prison. They were stoned; they were sawed in two; they were put to death by the sword. They went about in sheepskins and goatskins, destitute, persecuted and mistreated—the world was not worthy of them. They wandered in deserts and mountains, and in caves and holes in the ground. These were all commended for their faith, yet none of them received what had been promised (*the first coming of Christ*). God had planned something better for us so that only together with us would they be made perfect."

These died with their faith secure in the promised Messiah, though He had not yet come. So Christians today must endure unto the end—until the day comes when Christ takes them to heaven as promised. This is the ultimate goal in the mind of the writer of Hebrews.

The important point he is making in Hebrews 6:15 regarding the birth of Isaac, however, is that Abraham patiently waited a long time for God to keep His word and still did not give up his faith in God's promise: "And so after waiting patiently, Abraham received what was promised."

Abraham's Experience

The original readers of Hebrews—Jewish Christians of New Testament times—fully understand what Paul means, since they are familiar with Abraham's biography and history. Many Christians today, however, lack this familiarity with the Old Testament and the details of Abraham's life.

When we read the history of Abraham in the Old Testament, especially in the Book of Genesis, we find that the original promise God made to Abraham about his son, Isaac, was made to him when Abraham was 75 years old (Genesis 12:4).

By the time Isaac is born, however, Abraham has reached 100 years of age. This means Abraham waited 25 long years before God kept His promise. But what is even more amazing is that Isaac was born after his mother, Sarah, had passed the age of childbearing.

Paul presents this in a most interesting way in Romans 4:16-21: "Therefore, the promise comes by faith (*the promise of salvation is by faith alone and nothing else. Genuine faith will produce good works. The works do not save us. They are the fruits of salvation*), so that it may be by grace and may be guaranteed to all Abraham's offspring—not only to those who are of the law (*the Jews*) but also to those who are of the faith of Abraham. He is the father of us all." The promise to Abraham is that all nations will be blessed through that one Seed, Jesus Christ.

In verses 17 and 18 he says: "As it is written: I have made you a father of many nations." Abraham is the Christians' father in the sight of God. Abraham believed fully in God—in the God who gives life to the dead and calls things that are not as though they were. Against all hope, Abraham believed and so became the father of many nations, just as he had been told: "So shall your offspring be."

The Christian's faith must be the faith of Abraham; not only must a Christian believe in Jesus Christ as Messiah and Savior, but that faith must endure until the very end. This is the message of this passage.

Verse 18 continues: "Against all hope, Abraham in hope believed and so became the father of many nations, just as it had been said to him, 'So shall your offspring be.'"

Verse 19 then adds, "Without weakening in his faith, he faced the fact that his body was as good as dead—since it was about a hundred years old—and that Sarah's womb was also dead. Yet he did not waver through unbelief regarding the promise of God, but was strengthened in his faith and gave glory to God, being fully persuaded that God had power to do what he had promised." God keeps His promises—no doubt about that. The question is whether or not the Christian's faith is maturing to the point that it becomes unshakeable.

Using the experience of Abraham, Paul encourages the readers of Hebrews to demonstrate the same kind of faith—a faith that never gives up believing God's promise, no matter what happens. Abraham held onto his faith in God's promise to the very end. The Christian must do the same.

Now, notice what Hebrews 6:16 says: "Men swear by someone greater than themselves, and the oath confirms what is said and puts an end to all argument."

In Bible days the swearing of an oath in the name of a higher being confirmed a promise, or a will, just as a notarized promissory note is legally binding today. In this same way, says Paul, the promise of salvation made by God in Christ was also accompanied by an oath. He did this to remove any shadow of a doubt about our salvation in Christ.

We read in Hebrews 6:17: "Because God wanted to make the unchanging nature of his purpose very clear to the heirs of what was promised, he confirmed it with an oath." Verse 13 adds, "When God made His promise to Abraham, since there was no one greater for him to swear by, he swore by himself."

Verse 18 explains: "God did this so that, by two unchangeable things in which it is impossible for God to lie, we who have fled to take hold of the hope offered to us may be greatly encouraged." The two unchangeable facts about salvation are: First, the promise of God, which never fails because God never lies; and second, the oath of God which guarantees that He will keep His promise.

The writer of Hebrews says that these realities should greatly encourage believers in their determination to endure unto the end. And on this same theme, Hebrews 6 ends with verses 19 and 20: "We have this hope as an anchor for the soul, firm and secure. It enters the inner sanctuary (*the very presence of God*) behind the curtain, where Jesus, who went before us, has entered on our behalf. He has become a high priest forever, in the order of Melchizedek."

In the harbor of Corpus Christi, Texas, are three exact replicas of the ships in which Christopher Columbus and his men sailed across the Atlantic to reach the New World. It is amazing today how small these three ships truly are—they appear to be miniatures, but they are exactly the same size as the originals.

The huge liner "Queen Mary" has passed through storms in which she has been tossed about like a stick of wood. Imagine what Columbus and his men must have gone through in their tiny ships.

As the final spiritual storm gathers force, Christians must have a faith solidly anchored on the rock, Jesus Christ. In Bible times, ships were not much larger than those sailed in by Columbus. When the sailors of those times faced a storm, they would throw down their anchor so the ship would not capsize and be lost.

Paul uses this illustration to tell us that the anchor of salvation must be based, not on human promises or successes in Christian living, but on the promised Word of God and what God accomplished for mankind in Jesus Christ.

Furthermore, faith must not be limited to what Christ did in His earthly mission, wonderful and complete as that was. During His earthly mission—birth, life, death, and resurrection—Jesus did indeed obtain salvation full and complete for all. But the Christian's faith must go beyond what Jesus did on earth and look at Christ in the heavenly Sanctuary, sitting in the very presence of God as High Priest for humanity. Jesus is on humanity's side from beginning to end—a fact that should be the source of great encouragement to Christians who may be tempted to say "What's the use?"

The whole purpose of this epistle is to strengthen the readers' faith. Christians then, and certainly today, need that unshakeable faith that Paul writes about so eloquently.

In concluding the study of this great passage, let us read what the writer of Hebrews says in Hebrews 8:1 and 2 about Christ, the great High Priest: "The point of what we are saying is this: We do have such a high priest, who sat down at the right hand of the throne of the Majesty in heaven, and who serves in the sanctuary, the true tabernacle set up by the Lord, not by man."

Christians must not give up their faith. It is everything they have. In Romans 8:35 Paul asks a question, "Who shall separate us from the love of Christ? Shall trouble or hardship or persecution or famine or nakedness or danger or sword?"

Christians face all these things because they still live in enemy territory. But Paul testifies, in so many words, "I am persuaded that nothing in heaven, nothing in earth, no human experience, nothing I go through can ever separate me from the love of God that was revealed in Jesus Christ." This is the kind of faith Christians must develop.

In Summary

It bears repeating: the righteousness by which Christians are saved is always in Christ. He is in heaven where no thief can go. But the faith that makes this righteousness effective in Christians resides in them. Yes, God will always keep His promise to redeem mankind in Jesus Christ. But God will not force this fulfilled salvation onto any human being. He has created mankind with free will; therefore, the good news of salvation in Jesus Christ demands a human response— the response of faith.

I pray that the faith of all Christians reading this chapter will endure to the end. The most valuable thing the Christian possesses is faith in Christ. All material things—buying power, bank accounts, possessions—will be burned up. The Bible is clear about this. But faith in Christ guarantees eternal salvation. When Christ comes to take us to heaven, we will enjoy eternity with Him. We must never, never give up our faith!

CHAPTER 11
Pre-eminence of Christ's Priesthood
Hebrews 7:1-28

Paul in Hebrews 5:10 introduces Christ as mankind's High Priest after the order of Melchizedek. He repeats the same thought in Hebrews 6:20. Now in Hebrews 7 He explains in detail the significance of this truth. Dwelling at such length on the fact that Christ is the High Priest after the order of Melchizedek proves how important it is to him.

Christians often underemphasize the role of Christ as their High Priest—a tendency we will better understand by the time we've completed this chapter.

Who is Melchizedek?

In Hebrews 7:1-3 Paul provides some information about Melchizedek: "This Melchizedek was king of Salem and priest of God Most High. He met Abraham returning from the defeat of the kings and blessed him, and Abraham gave him a tenth of everything. First, his name means 'king of righteousness;' then, also, 'king of Salem' means 'king of peace', Without father or mother, without genealogy, without beginning of days or end of life, like the Son of God he remains a priest forever."

To understand what the apostle is describing here, we need some historical background. The Jews for whom Hebrews was specifically written were very familiar with the biblical figure Melchizedek. The story is much less well known today, so let us look at Genesis 14:1-11. In this passage, Moses describes the battle between the combined armies of four tribal kings and an alliance of five other tribal kings. It is a large, fierce battle and in course of the confrontation, Abraham's nephew Lot's family is taken prisoner from its home in Sodom.

Moving forward in the story as recounted in Genesis 14:13-16, we read that Abraham comes to the rescue of his nephew's family and that God gives him a great victory over the group of four kings that had initially defeated the other five. Then two men approach Abraham.

The first is the king of Sodom, who offers Abraham a large amount of material wealth in gratitude for his military assistance. In Genesis 14:17-24, then, we read that the second man greets Abraham—Melchizedek, king of Salem—who offers Abraham not material wealth but bread and wine.

But this Melchizedek is also priest of the Most High God—he is more than a king. The king of Sodom, who offered to shower Abraham with great wealth, represents the riches of this world, while Melchizedek, who blessed Abraham with bread and wine, represents God's supreme gift to the human race, Jesus Christ.

Every human being today is faced with these two alternatives. The Gift of God is Jesus Christ, while Satan dangles the promise of material blessings to distract us from the Gift of God.

Blessing of Bread and Wine

The blessing of bread and wine represents Jesus Christ, the Supreme Gift of God to mankind. We see here a connection to the Lord's Supper in which Jesus offers His disciples bread and wine and tells them to remember Him and His sacrifice every time they eat bread and drink wine.

The bread represents the perfect obedience of Christ in meeting the positive demands of the law, while the wine represents His life that was shed for the remission of sins. Both the "doing" and the "dying" of Christ are represented by the bread and wine.

With this understanding, let us read what Jesus tells His disciples in John 6:53-59: "Jesus said to them (*the Jews*), "I tell you the truth, unless you eat the flesh of the Son of Man and drink his blood, you have no life in you." Jesus continues, "Whoever eats my flesh and drinks my blood (*symbolized by the bread and the wine*) has eternal life, and I will raise him up at the last day. For my flesh is real food and my blood is real drink. Whoever eats my flesh and drinks my blood remains in me, and I in him."

Notice that the Lord's Supper is a symbol of a Christian's confession of faith in Jesus Christ: "Just as the living Father sent me and I live because of the Father, so the one who feeds on me will live because of me. This is the Bread that came down from heaven. Your forefathers ate manna and died, but he who feeds on this bread will live forever. He said this while teaching in the synagogue at Capernum."

Melchizedek, a priest of the Most High, offered Abraham bread and wine as symbols of the eternal life promised by God. According to Romans 4:16-25 and Galatians 3:6-14, Abraham represents the true Christian who puts his faith in Christ as his only hope of salvation, rather than on the material blessings of this world.

With this background, let us return to Hebrews 7 to study more about Christ as the great High Priest after the order of Melchizedek—a representative of Jesus Christ.

Tithing

In the first two verses of Hebrews 7 we note that after Melchizedek has blessed Abraham, the patriarch gives him a tenth of everything: "This Melchizedek was king of Salem and priest of God Most High. He met Abraham returning from the defeat of the kings and blessed him, and Abraham gave him a tenth (*tithe*) of everything."

Giving a tenth or tithe of everything to God's priest, or church, acknowledges one's total dependence on God. Tithing acknowledges that God is the rightful owner of everything a Christian possesses. Because they have been bought—not with silver or gold, but with the precious blood of the Lord, Jesus Christ—and are the purchased property of Christ, everything belongs to Him. This is the meaning of tithe paying, a practice first instituted by God in the Old Testament and never discontinued. A person does not pay tithe to earn salvation but as a confession of faith that he or she belongs to God.

The world we live in runs on money. Paul writes in 1 Timothy 6:10 that the love of money is the root of all evil and that in coveting money, some have drifted from their faith.

The Meaning of Names

The name Melchizedek means "King of Righteousness", and was the king of a city named Salem—which means "Peace". Later, Salem was renamed Jerusalem.

Abraham means "Father of the Faithful", and when we put the whole story together, we find that Abraham represents all believers who put their trust in God's gift of righteousness, Jesus Christ, rather than materialism. Abraham was offered two gifts—material blessings from the king of Sodom and spiritual blessings from the king of Salem. He chose the blessings of the bread and wine. True Christians still follow his example.

Melchizedek's Ancestry

The Bible is silent about the genealogy of Melchizedek—and this has a special meaning for the Jews of Paul's day. Genealogy is important to them, and the fact that Melchizedek is given no genealogy—no father, no mother in the historical record—suggests that he is eternal, changeless, his life and priesthood unending. This is why Paul compares Christ's priesthood to that of Melchizedek rather than to that of the Levites. We read in Hebrew 7:3: "Without father or without mother, without genealogy, without beginning of days or end of life, like the Son of God who remains a priest forever."

Believers in Jesus are daily and continually bombarded by Satan and his fiery darts, but the righteousness of Christ continually covers them as He intercedes for them against Satan's accusations.

While they live the Christian life, believers receive the peace that passeth understanding that Christ left with His followers when He ascended into heaven to sit at the right hand of God as humanity's great High Priest in the heavenly Sanctuary.

Superior to Levi

Once Paul has established this glorious truth, he continues to show that Christ as High Priest is superior to the Levitical priesthood of the Old Testament. Just as Melchizedek was superior to Levi from whom the Levitical priesthood sprung, so Christ is superior to the Levitical priesthood because He is High Priest after the order of Melchizedek.

Hebrews 7:4-10 begins: "Just think how great he was: Even the patriarch Abraham gave him a tenth of the plunder!" Paul clearly is referring to Melchizedek and continues: "Now the law requires that descendants of Levi who become priests to collect a tenth from the people—that is, their brothers—even though their brothers are descended from Abraham. This man (*Melchizedek*), however, did not trace his descent from Levi, yet he collected a tenth from Abraham (*the father of the Jews*) and blessed him who had the promises. And without doubt the lesser person is blessed by the greater. In the one case, the tenth is collected by men who die; but in the other case, by him who is declared to be living. One might even say that Levi, who collects the tenth, paid the tenth through Abraham, because when Melchizedek met Abraham, Levi was still in the body of his ancestor."

Some elements of the passage may be difficult for the Western mind to readily grasp, for Paul is using the argument of solidarity—the idea of corporate oneness. The Bible clearly endorses three major points based on solidarity: First, that God created all men in one man, Adam; Second, that Satan ruined the whole human race in that one man, Adam; and third, that God redeemed the whole human race in the second Adam, Jesus Christ.

Just as God created all men in one man, He also incorporated the whole human race in one man, the second Adam, Jesus Christ. Christ was not one man among many. As Savior, He is the whole human race in one Person. Jesus was a corporate Man. He was the second Adam. "Adam" in Hebrew means mankind (See Genesis 5:1,2).

Paul is telling the Jews in this passage that Abraham paid tithe to Melchizedek while Levi (*his great-grandson to be*) was still in Abraham's loins, or body. In this sense, then, Levi is participating in the act of paying tithe to Melchizedek. In return Melchizedek blesses Abraham.

Now, tithe-paying is generally seen as an admission that the one who pays the tithe is inferior to the one who receives it. In paying tithe to Melchizedek, Abraham is admitting that Melchizedek is superior to him. And since Levi is a part of Abraham's genetic body, Levi is likewise inferior. Paul is simply saying that Christ as High Priest is superior to the Levitical priesthood on which Judaism depended for intercession. Paul urges his readers not to give up on Christ as their High Priest or return to Judaism and dependence on the inferior, Levitical priesthood.

With this in mind, Paul continues in Hebrews 7:11-28, giving several reasons why Melchizedek is superior to Levi, as he shows that Christ's priesthood surpasses the Levitical priesthood. These verses have much less significance to Christians who no longer depend on the Levitical priesthood or are attracted to Judaism. But they contain at least five significant theological points of vital interest to readers today.

The Levitical Priesthood

The first point Paul makes is that if the Levitical priest were perfect, there would be no need for a supplementary priesthood. There would have been no call whatever for a priesthood according to the order of Melchizedek (verse 11). But because the Levitical priesthood was imperfect, another priesthood was needed.

His second point is that since a better priesthood is needed, our understanding of the Levitical priesthood needs to change. According to Jewish law, a priest has to be a descendant of Levi. But Christ was born of the tribe of Judah and has no standing within the Levitical order. But Christ's priesthood is still legitimate, for the Levitical priesthood consists of a dynasty whose members die and have to be replaced by other members of the Levitical clan. But Christ's priesthood, after the order of Melchizedek, is based upon an indestructible principle of priesthood that predates the Levitical and has no beginning and no end (verses 12-17).

Paul's third point is that the Levitical priesthood is weak, since it was established by a law that was incapable of producing perfection or righteousness in sinful flesh. In Romans 8:3 Paul says that what the law could not do, God did in Christ. The law could not produce righteousness. The law could not save sinners. That is why, incidentally, the High Priest who entered the Most Holy Place in the yearly Day of Atonement service of the earthly Sanctuary had to offer a sacrifice both for himself and his family. The priest himself, after all, was a sinner. Christ, however, did not have to offer a sacrifice for Himself because He was a better Priest— a perfect Priest. This is why mankind can now approach God directly through Christ, without fear or insecurity (Hebrews 7:18, 19).

The fourth point about the Levitical priesthood is that it was not established by an oath of permanence. Christ's priesthood, on the other hand, was sealed and established by an oath from God. This makes Christ's eternal priesthood a better priesthood than the Levitical.

The fifth point that highlights the inferiority of the Levitical priesthood is that the priests of that dynasty died and had to be replaced—proving that they were themselves sinners and subject to the wages of sin. In contrast, Christ's priesthood is a permanent one, since He has conquered death.

After offering a perfect sacrifice on the cross for mankind's sins, Christ conquered the grave and ascended to heaven to intercede as a great High Priest. His priesthood gives mankind the legal right to approach God with full confidence. What foolishness, then, to give up Christ! How foolish to revert to Judaism!

And how foolish for Christians today to give up Christ and go back to the world! This is what Demas does, as Paul mentions in 2 Timothy 4. Paul's great concern—and God's concern—is that Christians not give up their faith in Jesus Christ.

It is not enough to simply begin with faith, says Paul; faith must endure to the end. The same truth that applied to Jewish believers of New Testament times applies today. To give up faith is to give up Christ. To give up Christ is to give up the righteousness of Christ that saves. In other words, to give up Christ is foolishness, since there is no other sacrifice—no other Mediator between a holy God and sinful man.

This is why the Epistle to the Hebrews places so much emphasis on holding onto faith—on not giving it up. Let it endure until the end, because as the end approaches, the devil will do his utmost to take the believers out of Christ.

Salvation is guaranteed as long as Christians holds fast in the faith. But if they turn their backs on Christ in unbelief, they forfeit what God has accomplished in Jesus Christ. We must never, never forget that mankind is created with a free will—that each individual has the option of rejecting Christ. God's will is that none should perish. God's purpose is that every human being should be saved. He has obtained this right for the whole human race in Jesus Christ—but He can save only those who accept the gift, by faith.

When God promised Abraham in His seed "all nations will be blessed" pronouncement, he excluded nobody. The whole family of Adam—the whole human race to which we belong—was redeemed in Christ. God has kept that promise, but that promise is a gift, and like any gift, it can be deliberately, persistently, and ultimately rejected.

Christians accept that gift, and as long as they remain believers, their salvation is guaranteed. But the moment they say "good-bye" to Christ, they also say "good-bye" to salvation.

It is my prayer that no Christian reading this book will ever give up the faith. Christians need to grow in grace. They need to grow in truth. They need to be established in Christ in such a way that their faith becomes unshakeable. For as long as they believe, their salvation is guaranteed.

We close with the inspired and inspiring words of Paul to young Timothy, "I know in whom I believe; He is able to save me to the uttermost. I have kept the faith; I have fought the fight and now there is a crown of righteousness waiting for me even though I am going to be martyred in a few weeks. Now there is a crown of righteousness waiting for me and not only for me but for everyone who loves His appearing" (See 2 Timothy 4:7,8).

CHAPTER 12

Christ—Priest of a Better Covenant
Hebrews 8:1-13

In Hebrews 7:27 Paul moves from the person of Christ as great High Priest to His supreme sacrifice on the cross, where He liberated humanity from condemnation.

This supreme sacrifice is the central focus of Hebrews 8-10. The cross of Christ stands at the very heart of the gospel message and is well worth our study, as it is seen to validate the priesthood of Christ, beginning with Hebrews 8:1-13.

Hebrews 8:1-13 says: "The point of what we are saying is this: We do have such a high priest, who sat down at the right hand of the throne of the Majesty in heaven, and who serves in the sanctuary, the true tabernacle set up by the Lord, not by man. Every high priest is appointed to offer both gifts and sacrifices, and so it was necessary for this one also to have something to offer. If he were on earth, he would not be a priest, for there are already men who offer the gifts prescribed by the law. They serve at a sanctuary that is a copy and shadow of what is in heaven. This is why Moses was warned when he was about to build the tabernacle: 'See to it that you make everything according to the pattern shown you on the mountain.' But the ministry Jesus has received is as superior to theirs as the covenant of which he is mediator is superior to the old one, and it is founded on better promises. For if there had been nothing wrong with that first covenant, no place would have been sought for another. But God found fault with the people and said: 'The time is coming, declares the Lord, when I will make a new covenant with the house of Israel and with the house of Judah. It will not be like the covenant I made with their forefathers when I took them by the hand to lead them out of Egypt, because they did not remain faithful to my covenant, and I turned away from them, declares the Lord. This is the covenant I will make with the house of Israel after that time, declares the Lord. I will put my laws in their minds and write them on their hearts. I will be their God, and they will be my people. No longer will a man teach his neighbor, or a man his brother, saying, 'Know the Lord,' because they will all know me, from the least of them to the greatest. For I will forgive their wickedness and will remember their sins no more." By calling this covenant "new," he has made the first one obsolete; and what is obsolete and aging will soon disappear."

In the first two verses of chapter eight, Paul sums up all he has been saying about the priesthood of Christ, saying that Jesus as High Priest sits at the right hand of God in the heavenly Sanctuary. Then, beginning with verse 3, He turns his attention to the sacrifice of Christ—that which qualifies Jesus to represent humanity in the heavenly sanctuary.

A prophet is one who *represents God before the people.* A priest does the exact opposite—he *represents the people before God.* According to Isaiah 59:2, humanity's sins have separated mankind from a holy God. God is a consuming fire for sin. For Christ to breach the gap between sinners and a holy God, He must be able to offer two things: gifts and a sacrifice that can reconcile sinners to God.

Hebrews 8:3 says: "Every high priest is appointed to offer both gifts and sacrifices, and so it was necessary for this one (*Christ*) also to have something to offer."

According to the pattern God gave Moses, every priest was appointed to offer two things to reconcile sinners to God. A priest had to have both a gift and a sacrifice.

Christ's Gift

What do a gift and a sacrifice symbolize in the plan of salvation in Christ? The *gift* that Christ offers to God is His perfect righteousness that met the positive demands of the law. We find this clearly expressed in Romans 5:17: "For if, by the trespass of the one man (*Adam*), death reigned through that one man, how much more will those who receive God's abundant provision of grace and of the gift of righteousness reign in life through the one man, Jesus Christ."

Notice that righteousness is a gift. This gift, of course, is Jesus' fulfillment of the spirit (*or positive demands*) of the law through His perfect life. The perfect gift of Christ's righteousness was symbolized in the earthly sanctuary by the law requiring that the slain lamb be spotless. The spotlessness of the lamb represented the perfect righteousness of Christ, which qualified Him to be sacrificed.

Jesus' Sacrifice

This brings us to the second requirement for a priest—that he have a *sacrifice*. Why? Because perfect obedience cannot cancel sins already committed. The law of God does not only demand perfect obedience but also declares, "The soul that sins, it must die" (Ezekiel 18:20).

All have sinned; all have come short of the glory of God (Romans 3:23). Therefore the law of God demands death. This is why in the sanctuary service the earthly priest had to offer animal sacrifices before he could enter into the tabernacle to intercede on behalf of God's people.

Leviticus 17:11 explains why this had to be: "For the life of a creature is in the blood, and I have given it to you to make atonement for yourselves on the altar; it is the blood that makes atonement for one's life." Now, turning to Hebrews 9:22, we read: "In fact, the law requires that nearly everything be cleansed with blood, and without the shedding of blood there is no forgiveness (*or remission*)."

The blood of Christ was human blood. It had no special detergent to cleanse humanity's sin. But the word "blood" in the Old Testament symbolizes *life*. It was the life of Christ laid down in death that met the requirements of the law and paid the wages of sin. By giving His life Jesus satisfied the justice of the law and was qualified to represent humanity in the heavenly sanctuary.

Now, turning to Hebrews 8:4 and 5, we learn that Christ could not have qualified as a priest in the earthly sanctuary, for He did not belong by birth to the Levitical lineage. But Paul reminds his readers that the earthly sanctuary and its services were merely a type, or shadow, of the real plan of salvation. The earthly sanctuary, in fact, was built specifically as a model of the real sanctuary: "If he (*Jesus*) were on earth, he would not be a priest for there are already men who offer the gifts prescribed by the law. They serve at a sanctuary that is a copy and shadow of what is in heaven. This is why Moses was warned when he was about to build the tabernacle: 'See to it that you make everything according to the pattern shown you on the mountain.'"

The sacrifice of Christ and His priestly ministry in the heavenly sanctuary is the original plan of salvation in action. Hence it is superior to the Levitical priesthood of the earthly Sanctuary. If this argument sounds somewhat arcane to modern minds, we must bear in mind that Paul is using it to strengthen the faith of Jewish believers of his day. Though some of Paul's arguments seem to make no sense on first reading, his purpose is valid. Christians today must develop an unshakeable faith. Believers today need faith that endures to the end.

Paul's basic point is that Christ's priestly ministry in the heavenly sanctuary is not only superior to the earthly sanctuary's, He is able through His intercession to actually save us. In the same way, the New Covenant is superior to the old one. We find this in Hebrews 8:6: "But the ministry Jesus has received is as superior to theirs as the covenant of which he is Mediator is superior to the old one, and it is founded on better promises."

Old and New Covenants

There is one overarching difference between the old and new covenants, though both were given by God. While the Old Covenant was a contract—an agreement between two parties—the New Covenant is a will made by God on behalf of the human race.

What was the Old Covenant contract? In the Old Covenant contract, God spelled out His law, the measuring stick of righteousness. And He said in so many words, "If you meet the demands of the law perfectly and continually, heaven is yours." The people in response said, "Yes, all that you have told us, we will do." So the Old Covenant was based on man's promise to obey the law in order to be saved.

In total contrast, the New Covenant is a will in which God promises to redeem mankind from the sin problem—totally, through His Son, Jesus Christ. Man is simply to accept it as a gift. The promise is God's will; the enjoyment is ours as we receive the gift.

Sinful man is incapable of keeping God's holy law—Paul makes this clear in Romans 8:7 where he says that human beings are enemies of God and are not subject to the law of God, neither can be. In view of this, it goes without saying that the Old Covenant was faulty. The fault was not with God's promise or with the law, but with the people. Hence, the need for a new and better arrangement—the New Covenant. This is what Paul is saying in Hebrews 8:7-9: "For if there had been nothing wrong with that first covenant, no place would have been sought for another. But God found fault with the people." Notice, the fault was with the people.

We continue reading in Hebrews 8:7-9, "The time is coming, declares the Lord, when I will make a new covenant with the house of Israel and with the house of Judah. It will not be like the covenant I made with their forefathers when I took them by the hand to lead them out of Egypt, because they did not remain faithful to my covenant, and I turned away from them, declares the Lord.

"This is the covenant I will make with the house of Israel after that time, (*that is, after they failed to keep the first covenant*) declares the Lord. I will put my laws in their minds and write them on their hearts. I will be their God, and they will be my people."

Education—Not Salvation

Because the Jews of the Exodus never grasped the utter sinfulness of their human natures, they failed to realize the whole purpose of the Old Covenant. When God entered into the Old Covenant, did He know that the Jews could not keep His law? The answer is, "Yes." He knows that mankind, both then and now, is incapable of keeping the law by itself. But the Israelites never learned this essential lesson. So we must conclude that God did not enter into the Old Covenant with the Israelites to save them, but to prepare them—to educate them—for the coming Messiah. He knew they could not keep the commandments, but He entered into the covenant to help them realize their need as sinners. This is why Paul says in Galatians 3:19 onward that the law is a schoolmaster—a guide—that leads to Christ, where all may be justified by faith.

The First Covenant is a response to a major, persistent problem all human beings face. We refuse, by nature, to admit that of ourselves we are 100 percent sinners. We read in Jeremiah 17:9: "The heart is deceitful above all things." It is not only desperately wicked but deceitful. And whom does it deceive most? Itself! That's why human beings cannot depend on their own feelings and personal opinions of themselves. Paul himself admits as much in Romans 7:7, where he says that the law is not at fault for the sin problem. The problem is with the sin that dwells within every human being.

He goes on to say that before he truly understood the spirit of the law, he thought he was righteous—that is, until he discovered that the law demands not only perfect obedience in action but perfect thoughts and desires, too.

He did not know, or understand, sin until he pondered what the law said about coveting. Coveting is not an act, but a cherished desire that contradicts the will of God. By refusing to admit their utter sinfulness, however, the Jews (just as the Gentiles today) reduced the holy law of God to human rules that they could manage to keep outwardly, and thus deceive themselves and others.

The same problem develops in every pagan religion. Each teaches salvation by works and each defines goodness in terms of what human beings can attain through self-discipline. But when Jesus was asked what the greatest commandment is in the Book of the Law, He said, "Love for God and love for man." His response has nothing to do with performance and everything to do with inner attitude—that is, the spirit.

What Good Thing. . . ?

One day a young man came to Jesus and asked, "What good thing must I do to be saved? Jesus answered, in so many words, "Why do you call Me good? If you want to be saved by being good—and only God is good—then you must keep the commandments. Love thy neighbor as thyself." When the young man discovered that it was humanly impossible for him to treat his neighbors as he treated himself, he went home sorrowfully (Matthew 19:16-22).

Having pointed out the futility of trying to save ourselves under the Old Covenant, Paul turns to the New Covenant and enumerates its four provisions in Hebrews 8:10-12. And since Christians are under the umbrella of the New Covenant, they must take these four points seriously.

Law Written on the Heart

The first provision of the New Covenant is that God says He "will put My laws in their minds and write them on their hearts" (Hebrews 8: 10). This tells us up-front that the New Covenant does not do away with the law. Paul is simply saying that in the first covenant, the law was given simply as a set of rules; in the New Covenant, however, God will make the law a desire of the heart. When God says He will write these things on the heart, we must understand that He is saying He will change the hearts of His people—providing new hearts in harmony with the law.

The laws of God are holy; they are just; they are righteous; they are good. This is what Paul says in Romans 7:12. The problem in the Old Covenant was that sinners' hearts remained incompatible with the law. But justified believers in Christ are promised that they will be given the desire to be in harmony with the law. They will bear the fruit of the Spirit—joy, peace, love, longsuffering, patience, and so on, which are all in harmony with the law of God (Galatians 5:22, 23).

A Fatherly God

God's second provision of the New Covenant is that in it He says "I will be their God and they will be My people." We find these words in the second half of Hebrews 8:10.

Under the Old Covenant, the people developed an image of God as a severe judge out to punish everyone who failed to keep His law. Under the New Covenant, however, Jesus teaches His followers to address God as "Dear Father" "Abba, Father" in Aramaic means "Dear Father". God is a Father who loves His children and showers them with all kinds of blessings.

Under the New Covenant, Christians are no longer aliens before God. They are much more than forgiven sinners; they have been adopted into the family of God as His sons and daughters.

We read in 1 John 3:1: "What manner of love God has bestowed upon us that we should be called the children of God" (NKJV). No matter what we are now, when He comes, we shall be like Him.

In Galatians 4:4 and 5 we read: "But when the time had fully come, God sent His Son, born of a woman, born under the law, to redeem those under law, that we might receive the full rights of sons." Under the New Covenant, Christians are God's people—they belong to the family of God as sons and daughters.

Running Toward God

In sharing the third provision of the New Covenant, Paul writes, "No longer will a man teach his neighbor or a man his brother, saying, 'Know the Lord,' because they will all know me. They will all know me from the least of them to the greatest" (Hebrews 8:11).

Christianity involves a loving relationship with the Father. Instead of running away from God as under the Old Covenant, Christians run toward Him under the New Covenant.

Under the Old Covenant, God was seen as fearsome and forbidding—which is precisely why Adam and Eve tried to hide when God came to see them after their rebellion.

Under the New Covenant, God and the believers enjoy a wonderful relationship of love. The New Covenant is truly better than the Old Covenant in that it uses God's love to bind us together and to Him. The relationship depends, not on our love for God but His love for us.

First John 4:16-18 says: "And so we know and rely on the love God has for us. God is love. Whoever lives in love lives in God, and God in him. In this way, love is made complete (*or perfect*) among us so that we will have confidence on the day of judgment, because in this world we are like him. There is no fear in love. But perfect love drives out fear, because fear has to do with punishment. The one who fears is not made perfect in love." Those still afraid of God are still living with Old Covenant attitudes.

Sins Forgotten

Under the New Covenant, God gives yet a fourth provision, promising, "I will forgive their wickedness (*their sins*) and will remember their sins no more." Christians are absolutely redeemed people.

Paul concludes this section of Hebrews by informing his readers that since the introduction of the New Covenant in Christ, the Old Covenant no longer applies. And he asks his readers to enjoy the New Covenant—not to return to the old, for it had no redemptive value. But in the New Covenant there is joy, peace, victory, and hope.

CHAPTER 13

The Heavenly Sanctuary
Hebrews 9:1-28

In Hebrews 9 and 10 the writer of Hebrews focuses on the Old Testament sanctuary and its services, as established by the Israelites according to God's instructions through Moses.

Why did God instruct the Israelites to make Him a place to dwell in their desert camp? Clearly, this was God's visual aid in presenting the total plan of salvation to these former slaves. So when we visualize the Old Testament sanctuary and its services, we are looking at God's model of salvation from beginning to end. We could call it His "Show and Tell."

The emphasis of the book of Hebrews and the rest of the New Testament in dealing with the sanctuary and its services, is not on buildings but on Christ. The sanctuary revealed to the Old Testament followers of God not only the earthly mission of redemption the Lord, Jesus Christ would undertake, but also his heavenly ministry where He intercedes on behalf of the believers.

We will now consider Hebrews 9, in which the writer tells his readers that a *heavenly* sanctuary supersedes the earthly sanctuary.

A Heavenly Sanctuary

Paul says in Hebrews 8:1 and 2 that after finishing His earthly ministry, Jesus ascended into heaven and sat at the right hand of God in the heavenly Sanctuary to intercede for His followers: "The point of what we are saying is this: We do have such a high priest, who sat down at the right hand of the throne of the Majesty in heaven, and who serves in the sanctuary, the true tabernacle set up by the Lord, not by man."

When we come to Hebrews 9 and 10, however, we suddenly face two entire chapters that present the contrast between the earthly sanctuary (a representation of the heavenly sanctuary) and the heavenly sanctuary itself (which is the reality of the plan of salvation).

John writes in John 1:14 that the Word was made flesh and dwelt among us. The Greek word actually means "tabernacled" among us, "And we beheld his glory, the glory of the only begotten of the Father, full of grace and truth" (NKJV). This statement fulfills Exodus 25:8, where God tells Moses, "Have them make a sanctuary for me, and I will dwell among them."

We discover in Hebrews 9 that the writer continues to address himself primarily to Jewish Christians. But its message also has special meaning for Christians today, for it says that when Christ finished His earthly mission, He did not go to the earthly sanctuary (Jewish temple) to intercede for His people but to the heavenly sanctuary. The two are distinct and different, for the earthly was a type—or symbol—of the heavenly, which encompasses the actual plan of salvation.

So as we study the sanctuary message as given in the Old Testament and explained in Hebrews 9 and 10 and elsewhere, we find that the emphasis is not in buildings, compartments, curtains, or animal sacrifices, but on Jesus Christ.

The Real Temple

In John 2:19 Jesus tells the Jews, "Destroy this temple, and I will raise it again in three days." The temple, built in Jerusalem, was an elaborate building in harmony with the first earthly sanctuary that God had told Moses how to build as a large, movable tent.

When Jesus spoke of destroying the temple and raising it back up in three days, the Jews immediately thought He was referring to the massive temple buildings of His day. But after Jesus' resurrection—Jesus rose, remember, on the third day after His death—the disciples realized that Jesus had not been talking about a building but about His body (See John 2:19-22).

The earthly sanctuary service was conducted by priests who themselves were sinners—which meant they could not enter directly into the presence of God. In the earthly sanctuary/temple, interestingly enough, there were two rooms, separated by a curtain. But as Jesus hung on the cross, that curtain was miraculously and literally ripped from top to bottom, signifying that Jesus on the cross was cleansing the human race of all sin (Mark 15:37-39). The cross was paying the price for the sins of the world. This is why Christians today, living in

New Testament times, can boldly come to God through the Lord, Jesus Christ—a reality Hebrews 9 and 10 eloquently brings out.

The Earthly Sanctuary

Let us now study Hebrews 9 closely to understand what parts of the sanctuary service Christ fulfilled in His earthly mission and what He is fulfilling today in His heavenly ministry.

In the first five verses of Hebrews 9 Paul gives a brief, general description of the earthly sanctuary—after all, the Jews to whom he was writing, already had a very clear picture of what the sanctuary looked like. But this summary helps those of us today who are not as familiar with the sanctuary, its message, and its services.

Hebrews 9:1-5 says: "Now the first covenant had regulations for worship and also an earthly sanctuary. A tabernacle was set up. In its first room were the lamp stand, the table and the consecrated bread; this was called the Holy Place. Behind the second curtain was a room called the Most Holy Place, which had the golden altar of incense and a gold-covered ark of the covenant. This ark contained the gold jar of manna, Aaron's staff that had budded, and the stone tablets of the covenant (*that is, the Ten Commandments*). Above the ark were the cherubim of the Glory, overshadowing the atonement cover (*or the mercy seat*). But we cannot discuss these things in detail now."

The writer of Hebrews is saying, in other words, "I am giving you a general description of the sanctuary, but I am not going to explain in every detail what these different furnitures symbolize."

In Hebrews 9:6 and 7 the writer goes on to describe the two main sanctuary services—the daily and the yearly: "When everything had been arranged like this, the priests entered regularly (*daily*) into the outer room to carry on their ministry. But only the high priest entered the inner room, and that only once a year, and never without blood, which he offered for himself and for the sins the people had committed in ignorance."

Paul is telling us here that the sanctuary was not only a building but had functions and services. In verse 8 he says that these services were to point to Christ: "The Holy Spirit was showing by this that the way into the Most Holy Place had not yet been disclosed as long as the first tabernacle was still standing."

In other words, the earthly sanctuary, with all its services, was a shadow—it was a type, or earthly forerunner, of the reality. As long as it existed, humanity possessed only a representation of the divine reality yet to come. But when Christ came—when He died on the cross and the temple curtain was ripped open by God's hand, from top to bottom—God was telling the Jews that the type and shadow had met its reality (Matthew 27:51).

Paul is saying here in Hebrews that Christ's heavenly ministry of intercession could not begin until He had finished His earthly mission—a mission that, when complete, fulfilled in reality the forms and types represented by the earthly sanctuary and its services.

In Hebrews 9:9 and 10, Paul goes on to remind us that everything about the earthly sanctuary—its building, its furniture, its services—were all symbolic and temporary. The earthly sanctuary, in other words, was a shadow or a type which had no power to save either Jew or Gentile from sin. It had no power to remove guilt, says Paul: "This is an illustration (*the earthly sanctuary which he described in brief in verses 1-8*) for the present time (*Old Testament times*), indicating that the gifts and sacrifices being offered were not able to clear the conscience of the worshiper. They are only symbolic food and drink and various ceremonial washings—external regulations applying until the time of the new order."

Jesus' Sanctuary Ministry

The earthly sanctuary was simply a visual aid God gave the Jews to remind them of the promise and function of the coming Messiah. As long as these symbols remained, it reminded them that the Messiah had not yet come. But Hebrews 9:11 and 12 now tells us that after Christ's death on the cross—in which He broke the hold of sin once and for all—He did not enter the earthly temple in Jerusalem to minister, but ascended to the heavenly sanctuary: "When Christ came as high priest of the good things that are already here, he went through the greater and more perfect tabernacle that is not man-made, that is to say, not a part of this creation. He did not enter by means of the blood of goats and calves; but he entered the Most Holy place (*that is, the very presence of God*) once for all by his own blood, having obtained eternal redemption."

These verses are highly significant, especially for those to whom Paul was writing. Bear in mind that the early Jewish Christians were being tempted to give up Christ and go back to the types and shadows of the Jewish sanctuary and its services. Paul is saying that to do this would be foolish—in fact meaningless. It would be like trading in one's completed house in exchange for a copy of its blueprints. The blueprints of a house are important—especially before the house is built. But once the house is built, the blueprints are filed away and do little more than collect dust.

Likewise, Paul is saying, when Christ came to this world and fulfilled what the sacrificial system of the earthly sanctuary foretold, He did not take His blood to the earthly sanctuary, but to heaven.

Verses 13 and 14 tell us clearly that the earthly sanctuary and its sacrifices gave no release from sin. But the reality of that sanctuary symbolism—the actual supreme sacrifice of Christ which satisfied the just demands of the law—does guarantee salvation to those who accept it by faith.

Sacrificial Animals

The animals sacrificed in the earthly sanctuary before Christ died on the cross were only a shadow—a type pointing forward to His sacrifice. These sacrifices had no power or legal right to forgive sinners. But the blood of Christ did.

Verses 13 and 14 tell us: "The blood of goats and bulls and the ashes of a heifer sprinkled on those who are ceremonially unclean sanctify them so that they are outwardly clean (*in other words, there is no reality in that cleansing, for it is simply a symbolic gesture*). How much more, then, will the blood of Christ, who through the eternal Spirit offered himself unblemished to God, cleanse our consciences from acts that lead to death, so that we may serve the living God!"

These two verses tell us that while the sacrificial system had no power to save, the blood of Christ has absolute power to save. In Romans 3:25 Paul tells us that before Christ died on the cross, God forgave sins only through His forbearance, because legally He had no right to forgive sins. Why? Because as we learn in Hebrews 9: 22, without shedding of blood there can be no remission of sins.

On the cross Jesus shed His blood for the forgiveness of our sins. On the cross the shadow was met by the reality, the type met antitype. And since the cross, God does have the legal right to forgive mankind (See Romans 3:26).

A Better Sacrifice

Now we turn to Hebrews 9:15-21 and Paul's conclusion that when believers depend on Christ as their Savior in the heavenly sanctuary, that this is far more effective than going back to Judaism and the ministry of the earthly priests.

We read in these verses (15-21) of the contrast between the Old Covenant (represented by the earthly sanctuary) and the New Covenant (represented by Christ). Unlike the Old Covenant, which was contractual, Paul compares the New Covenant to a will made by God, in Christ. Since Christ's death, this is no longer a promise but a reality: "For this reason Christ is the mediator of a new covenant, that those who are called may receive the promised eternal inheritance—now that he has died as a ransom to set them free from the sins committed under the first covenant. In the case of a will, it is necessary to prove the death of the one who made it (*as we well know, a will does not become effective until the person who makes the will dies because a will goes into force only after*) somebody has died; it never takes effect while the one who made it is living. This is why even the Old Covenant included blood in its inauguration service. After Moses had proclaimed every commandment of the law to all the people, he took the blood of calves with water, scarlet wool, and branches of hyssop and sprinkled the scroll and all the people. He said, "This is the blood of the covenant, which God has commanded you to keep."

Likewise, Moses sprinkled blood on the sanctuary tabernacle and everything used in its ceremonies. The law, in fact, requires that nearly everything be cleansed with blood, for "without the shedding of blood there is no forgiveness."

Remember what Jesus did when He introduced the Lord's Supper. He took the cup, blessed it, and said, "This is My blood shed for the remission of sins."

This is what verse 22 is saying—that without shedding of blood there can be no remission of sin. Even so, there is much confusion among Christians today about how this verse pertains to the blood of Christ. When the Bible teaches in the New Testament that by the shedding of Christ's blood all are cleansed of sin, we must not take that statement about "blood" literally. Instead we must turn back to the Old Testament and refresh our understanding of the meaning of "blood." Here we learn that "blood" simply represents "life."

The text that brings this out most clearly is Leviticus 17:11, where we learn that it is "life" shed for the remission of sin that cleanses from all sin. The word "blood" is symbolic of "life." It is symbolic because the literal blood of Christ was no different from our human blood. We read in Hebrews 2:14 onward that just as the Jews were partakers of flesh and blood, Christ took part of the same. The physical blood of Christ was no different than ordinary human blood. In this context, then, let us read Leviticus 17:11: "For the life of a creature is in the blood, and I have given it to you to make atonement for yourselves on the altar; it is the blood that makes atonement for one's life."

Blood symbolizes life and shed blood symbolizes life laid down in death—exactly what took place at the cross. On the cross Jesus laid down His life for the sins of the world. On the cross Jesus met the just demands of the law because the law says, "The soul that sins, the life that sins, it must die" (Ezekiel 18:20).

Jesus did not come to change the death sentence; He came to fulfill it so that He might be just and the justifier of everyone who believes. This is exactly what Hebrews 9:23-29 is pointing out: "It was necessary, then, for the copies of the heavenly things to be purified with these sacrifices (*that is, of animals*), but the heavenly things themselves with better sacrifices than these. For Christ did not enter a man-made sanctuary that was only a copy of the true one; he entered heaven itself, now to appear for us in God's presence. Nor did he enter heaven to offer himself again and again, the way the high priest enters the Most Holy Place every year with blood that is not his own. Then Christ would have had to suffer many times since the creation of the world. But now he has appeared once for all at the end of the ages to do away with sin by the sacrifice of himself. Just as man is destined to die once, and after that to face judgment, so Christ was sacrificed once to take away the sins of many people; and he will appear a second time, not to bear sin, but to bring salvation to those who are waiting for him."

What this passage is telling us is that in the earthly sanctuary service, the priest offered animals—not only daily but yearly. Yearly he offered the goats; daily he offered the lambs. Paul is saying to his Jewish readers that the reason there was a continual need of offerings is that the blood of these animals did not legally remove sin. But when Jesus died on the cross, He paid the price for the sins of the whole human race from Adam to the last human being, for Christ was the Second Adam. He died as if the whole human race had died. He bore us on the cross. This is why 2 Corinthians 5:14 says that when one died, all died. First Peter 2:24 says that He bore our sins in His body. He bore us and by bearing us He bore our sins. The one sacrifice of Christ on the cross was sufficient for the sins of the whole human race for all time.

Those who accept Christ and who are looking forward to His Second Coming are told that Christ will no longer come to deal with the sin problem—that was dealt with at the cross. The salvation Christ obtained for the entire human race in His earthly mission was full and complete. When Christ comes the second time, He will have already dealt with it fully and completely by His life and death.

Neither He nor we can add to it; we cannot improve on it, so we must never try to add to it by our own good works. Even the work of the Holy Spirit in us does not contribute toward that salvation, for the Holy Spirit is not a Co-redeemer with Christ. He is simply the Communicator of the salvation that Christ already obtained for mankind in His earthly mission.

The Second Coming of Christ, then, is a blessed hope only to those who accept Christ as their complete Savior. If any of us has not accepted Christ, it is still not too late. The Second Coming of Christ is the wrath of God only to those who do not believe. But to those who believe it is the blessed hope. This is *my* hope for all of us, in Jesus' name.

CHAPTER 14

Christ's Perfect Sacrifice

Hebrews 10:1-22

Last chapter we studied Hebrews 9, where the writer introduces us to the sanctuary service God gave Moses during the Exodus, as a visual aid for the actual plan of salvation in Christ.

In Hebrews 9 we see that the cross fulfills what is foreshadowed by the Old Testament sanctuary service. At the heart of the gospel message is the cross of Christ.

When Paul writes to the Corinthian Christians, he says in 1 Corinthians 1:17,18: "For Christ did not send me to baptize, but to preach the gospel—not with words of human wisdom, lest the cross of Christ be emptied of its power. For the message of the cross is foolishness to those who are perishing, but to us who are being saved (*that is, believers*) it is the power of God."

Christ's shed blood on the cross is what gives the believers the legal right to go to heaven. We read in Hebrews 9:22: "Without shedding of blood there is no remission of sins" (NKJV). The shedding of animals' blood in the Old Testament sanctuary points to Jesus' life spilled out on the cross. As Jesus blesses the cup at His Last Supper, he says "this cup represents my blood which was shed for the remission of sins."

The apostle John in 1 John 1: 9 says, "If we confess our sins, he (*Jesus, God*) is faithful and just and will forgive us of our sins and purify us from all unrighteousness." This leads us directly to the theme of Hebrews 10.

The Significance of Blood

In this study we look at the first half of Hebrews 10. But first let us review the significance of the word "blood." When the New and Old Testaments use the word "blood", the reference is not to the literal blood of Christ poured out through His pierced hands, forehead, side, and feet. As we read in Leviticus 17:11, blood represents *life*. In the

New Testament, the phrase "blood of Christ,"or "Christ shed His blood for us," always refers to the life of Christ, which He laid down in death for mankind's sins.

The law of God says "The soul that sins, it must die." Jesus did not come to commute that death sentence, for that would have made Him transgressor of His own law. What He did was come to *fulfill* that death sentence—Himself. At the incarnation He took upon Himself human nature. On the cross He surrendered that humanity in death, paying the wages of sin on behalf of the human race He had created. The sacrificing of the human life of Christ is what the New Testament is talking about when it refers to the blood of Christ.

To clearly bring this into focus, let us read John 10:11: "I (*Jesus referring to Himself*) am the good shepherd. The good shepherd lays down his life for the sheep." Then in John 15:13 we read, "Greater love has no one than this, that he lay down his life for his friends (*Jesus speaking to His disciples*)."

Whenever we read "the blood of Christ,"it clearly refers to Jesus' life, laid down for the sins of the world.

With this understanding of the phrase "the blood of Christ," we are ready to look closely at the first half of Hebrews 10.

A Better Sacrifice

Chapter 10 contrasts animal sacrifices to the sacrifice of Christ. The animal sacrifices had no power to save, Paul says, but Christ's sacrifice can cleanse humanity of all sin.

In Hebrews 10:1-4, Paul reminds his Jewish readers that the blood of animals cannot save them from their sins, since these are only a shadow of Jesus' sacrifice: "The law is only a shadow of the good things that are coming—not the realities themselves. For this reason it can never, by the same sacrifices repeated endlessly year after year, make perfect those who draw near to worship. If it could, would they not have stopped being offered? For the worshipers would have been cleansed once for all, and would no longer have felt guilty for their sins. But those sacrifices are an annual reminder of sins, because it is impossible for the blood of bulls and goats to take away sins."

This is something we all know, as Christians. These animal sacrifices are only a shadow, or type. Animal life can never take the place of human life. Nor does the law allow the guilt and punishment of one sinner to pass to be charged to an innocent surrogate. This is why the humanity of Christ *was* corporate humanity's—even as Adam's humanity contained the humanity of all of his descendants.

A text that most clearly pronounces sin non-transferable is found in Deuteronomy 24:16: "Fathers (*writes Moses*) shall not be put to death for their children, nor children put to death for their fathers; each is to die for his own sin." This is a fundamental principle of good law.

Back in 1986, for example, a young man named Ted Bundy was executed for committing multiple murders. Before he was put to death, however, his mother announced that she was willing to die in her son's place. But the laws of the United States of America would not allow this substitution. The judge said, "No."

Likewise, animal blood cannot legally pay the price for the sins of the human race, as the first four verses of Hebrews 10 clearly state. How, then, can God solve this ethical problem of the law, of salvation, and the gospel?

God solved the sin problem by first qualifying Christ to be mankind's true Substitute. We have substitute teachers; we have substitutes in basketball, in football, in soccer. But not just anyone can be a substitute teacher, for example. A person has to be trained as a teacher to be able to substitute for another teacher. A person must be an expert or have great proficiency in a position for which he or she is substituting. Likewise, God had to qualify Christ to be mankind's Substitute. How did He do it?

He did this in the incarnation when He, through the Holy Spirit, united the divinity of Christ with mankind's corporate, as-yet-unredeemed humanity. This made Christ the Second Adam and legally qualified Him to represent mankind in His redemptive mission.

Just as all humanity sinned in Adam and stands condemned in Adam, God made it possible for Adam and his descendants to obey in Christ so that they could be justified and receive eternal life in Him. This is set forward in Hebrews 2, especially verses 9-15. The same truth now reappears in Hebrews 10:5-10, but with a different approach and more detail.

The writer of Hebrews says in this passage: "Therefore (*in view of the fact that animal sacrifices cannot truly deal with the sin problem),* when Christ came into the world, he said: 'Sacrifice and offering you did not desire.'"

Christ did not come to perpetuate the sacrificial system but to become the reality of those sacrifices. The passage continues, "'But a body you prepared for me (*a human body prepared in the womb of Mary containing the complete life of the as-yet-unredeemed human race*).'"

Verse 6 continues: "With burnt offerings and sin offerings you were not pleased. Then I said, 'Here I am—it is written about me in the scroll—I have come to do your will, O God.' First he said, 'Sacrifices and offerings, burnt offerings and sin offerings you did not desire, nor were you pleased with them.'"

Why was God not pleased with the very sacrificial system He had given to the Jews in the Old Testament? The answer is that it was simply a visual aid—not the real thing. But this did not stop some from assuming that the visual aid was the reality. Hebrews here makes it abundantly clear: The sacrifice of animals had no power to save humanity. Salvation comes only from the sacrifice of Christ.

Verses 9 and 10 continue: "Then he (*Jesus*) said, 'Here I am, I have come to do your will.' He sets aside the first (*the shadow, the Old Covenant*) to establish the second (*the reality which is the New Covenant*). And by that will, we have been made holy through the sacrifice of the body of Jesus Christ once for all."

How wonderful to know that in Jesus Christ we have already been made holy—not just forgiven, wonderful as that is. Believers are actually made righteous—made holy—so that they stand perfect before God in their Lord, Jesus Christ.

This is why those who have not accepted Christ are making a great mistake, for they are dealing not with things of their world, but with eternity. What we must recognize is that many of the words and thoughts of Hebrews 10:5-7 come from Psalm 40, where David predicts the coming of Christ. But because Paul is writing to Jews who knew Psalm 40 by heart from singing it in their synagogues, he does not quote the entire passage.

But it will help us in our study if we quote the whole passage here: "Sacrifice and offering you did not desire, but my ears you have pierced, burnt offerings and sin offerings you did not require. Then I said, 'Here I am, I have come—it is written about me in the scroll. I desire to do your will, O my God; your law is within my heart.'"

The will of God was to redeem mankind, but He cannot justify sinners unless He meets the full demands of the law. And that is what Jesus came to accomplish and this is what He did. Hebrews 10:11 and 12 points out that since Christ's death on the cross, Jesus did not once enter the earthly temple to minister but ascended to the heavenly Sanctuary to represent humanity through His perfect life and sacrificial death.

The passage reads: "Day after day every priest stands and performs his religious duties; again and again he offers the same sacrifices, which can never take away sins. But when this priest had offered for all time (*referring to Christ*) one sacrifice for sins, he sat down at the right hand of God."

When Christ came to this earth 2,000 years ago, He came as the Lamb of God that taketh away the sins of the world. When He returned to the Father and sat at His right hand in the heavenly Sanctuary, He came as humanity's Priest. The word "priest" means somebody who represents the congregation before God. It is the opposite of a prophet, for a prophet represents God *before the people*, while a priest *represents the people before God*.

After having redeemed mankind fully by His life and death, Christ returned to heaven to intercede on our behalf. Mankind needs an intercessor because, though Christians are perfect in Christ, they are still sinners in and of themselves. Martin Luther was absolutely right when he told his listeners that Christians—believers—are simultaneously sinners and righteous. They are 100 percent sinners and 100 percent righteous at the same time. They are sinners in and of themselves but righteous in Christ. This is what the gospel is all about—the good news of salvation.

In Hebrews 10:15-21 we continue reading: "The Holy Spirit also testifies to us about this. First he says: 'This is the covenant I will make with them after that time, says the Lord. I will put my laws in their hearts, and I will write them on their minds.' Then He adds: 'Their sins and lawless acts I will remember no more. And where they have been forgiven, there is no longer any sacrifice for sin.' Therefore, brothers, since we have confidence to enter the Most Holy Place (*that is, the very presence of God*) by the blood of Jesus, by a new and living way opened for us through the curtain, that is, his body, and since we have a great priest over the house of God, let us draw near to God with a sincere heart in full assurance of faith, having our hearts sprinkled to cleanse us from a guilty conscience and having our bodies washed with pure water. Let us hold unswervingly to the hope we profess, for he who promised is faithful."

Paul is saying that as long as the believers depend on Christ as their Mediator in the heavenly sanctuary, they can be absolutely sure of their salvation.

For the early Christian Jews to go back to Judaism, and for Christians living in the 21st century to give up their faith in Christ, would therefore be a great mistake.

The New Covenant

Note the contrast between the Old Covenant (represented by the earthly sanctuary) and the New Covenant (represented by Christ). Unlike the Old Covenant, which was a contractual agreement in which God gave the law and men had to keep it to be saved, the New Covenant is compared to a will made by God in Christ. Christ's death made the will effective. In this New Covenant God does not only offer to redeem mankind from every aspect of the sin problem, but He writes the law in the believers' hearts. This simply means that He puts God's unconditional, self-emptying love and spirit of His law into the believers' hearts. This changes desires, motives, and direction of life. Those who receive this infilling now want to do the will of God, in harmony with the law of God. This is the distinction between works of the law and works of faith. Works of the law means keeping the law as a means of salvation, motivated by egocentric concerns. The gospel does not do away with the law. It does away with human beings *being under the law* and offers the believers a New Covenant. In that New Covenant the law can be written in their hearts so that it is no longer a requirement but their desire to keep it, because of the love of Christ that constrains them.

In verses 22 and 23 Paul points out a fundamental truth about the law. Only the shedding of blood—life laid down in death—can legally forgive sin, for the Lord has declared that the wages of sin is death (Romans 6:23).

In the same way, the heavenly Sanctuary has to be cleansed by blood—not the blood of animals but the blood of Christ. Hebrews 10: 23-25 addresses this question: "Let us hold unswervingly the hope we profess, for He who promises is faithful. And let us consider how we may spur one another towards love and good deeds. Let us not give up meeting together, as some are in the habit of doing, but let us encourage one another—and all the more as you see the Day approaching."

Paul is saying that the only way to approach God is through the shed blood of Jesus Christ. He is reminding the New Testament Jews that to go back to Judaism would be to turn their backs on their only hope of salvation. In Hebrews 10:14 we read: "Because by one sacrifice he has made perfect forever those who are being made holy."

In Hebrews 10:24-29 the writer says that if the believers turn their backs on the sacrifice of Christ, they have nothing to face but the judgment. "If we deliberately keep on sinning,"he says, meaning that if believers deliberately keep on rejecting Christ after they have received the knowledge of the truth—after they have realized and understood and been convicted of the truth of the gospel (Verse 26-29)—"no sacrifice for sin is left, but only a fearful expectation of judgment and of raging fire that will consume the enemies of God. Anyone who rejected the law of Moses died without mercy on the testimony of two or three witnesses. How much more severely do you think a man deserves to be punished who has trampled the Son of God underfoot, who has treated as an unholy thing the blood of the covenant that sanctified him, and who has insulted the Spirit of grace?"

These are strong words. The writer of Hebrews is saying that if, under the law, one can be punished when two or three witnesses declares him guilty, how much more those deserve to be punished who deliberately, persistently, and ultimately reject the gift of salvation?

For believers to reject Christ is inexcusable because His salvation is a gift—a gift that costs them nothing but cost God an infinite price.

To give up this wonderful gospel—to give up this hope of salvation in Christ, to give up the cross—is the greatest mistake any human being can make. When Christ comes the second time, He will come not to deal with the sin problem, for He has already dealt with it at His First Coming. The salvation Christ obtained for the human race in His earthly mission was full and complete. Believers must never turn their backs on this salvation and must sincerely ask God to give them strength because, as long as they are in Christ, there is no condemnation (Romans 8:1).

The believers have peace with God only through justification by faith (Romans 5:1).

CHAPTER 15
The Cost of Unbelief
Hebrews 10:23-39

Our study this chapter takes us from Hebrews 10:23 to verse 29— a short but extremely important passage that deals with the high cost of unbelief.

This study bases itself on the inspired concept that redemption has been obtained completely and perfectly in Jesus Christ for *all* humanity—subject to their acceptance of that redemption, by faith.

Four Important Points

Our study so far of Hebrews 10 can be summed up by four important points. The first is that in the body God prepared for Christ, type met antitype. Jesus *became* the human race—His body represents everyone who has ever lived or will live, even as Adam's body contained the hereditary material of every human being who has lived or ever will live. Christ is called the Second Adam, or the Last Adam—and rightly so, for the name "Adam" means "Mankind". Christ, our Creator, became "Mankind" (See 1 Corinthians 15:45-49).

Jesus' life and death fulfilled all that was promised by the Old Testament sanctuary service. Christ satisfied all the demands of the law, thus obtaining for mankind full and complete salvation. The writer of Hebrews spells this out in the first 10 verses of Chapter 10.

This study's second important point is that unlike the repeated sacrifices of the sanctuary service, Christ's perfect redemption has been completed, once and for all for the human race—from Adam to the last human being born on earth. On the cross when Jesus cried, "It is finished,"He expressed a truth brought out in Hebrews 10:14: "Because by one sacrifice (*that is, the cross of Christ*) he has made perfect forever those who are being made holy." In Christ salvation is full and complete (Hebrews 10:11-14).

The third important point is found in Hebrews 10:15-18. Here we discover that the finished work of Christ not only leads to full assurance of salvation but to the law being written in believers' hearts. This fulfills, of course, the New Covenant promise God makes in the Old Testament (Jeremiah 31:31-34).

The fourth and final point, found in Hebrews 10:19-22, says that the believers stand perfect in Christ and can approach the very presence of God, boldly and with full assurance of salvation. This is what makes the gospel such good news.

A Misunderstanding

In view of these facts, the writer of Hebrews warns his readers of the danger of denying their faith in Christ, and he continues explaining this warning throughout this study.

But before we tackle this subject, we need to clarify a problem—a misunderstanding—held by many Christians. This is a belief in "once saved, always saved." The argument goes like this: Once a person has accepted Christ and has become part of the family of Christ, he or she can never lose salvation. In other words, once a person is adopted into the family of Christ, they remain family members forever.

Ordinarily this is true. But keep in mind that if a son or daughter leaves his family home and deliberately tells his mother and father, "I want nothing more to do with you; I want nothing to do with what you have and what is mine by inheritance."

If a son or daughter disowns the family and all the family stands for, all family benefits and privileges are lost.

Scripture nowhere teaches that salvation can never be lost. True, as long as believers remain under the umbrella of justification by faith, they have full assurance of salvation. But the righteousness that saves them—the righteousness that qualifies them for heaven, now and in the judgment—is always in Christ. And He is, at this moment, in heaven where no thief can enter and rob Him of that righteousness. But the faith that makes that righteousness ours—the faith that makes the righteousness of Christ effective in us as individuals—is not in Christ but *in us*.

We still are living on earth—in Satan's territory—and Satan can touch that faith. We will find in this study that believers who deliberately and irrevocably abandon their faith in Christ also forfeit all the blessings God has obtained for them in Christ.

Let Us Be Firm

With these things in mind, we turn to Hebrews 10:23 and read, "Let us be firm and unswerving in the confession of our hope, for the Giver of the promise may be trusted" (NEB). Since it is possible to lose salvation by renouncing faith, Paul earnestly pleads with his readers to hold firmly to their faith in Christ to the very end. Otherwise, God's hands are tied; He cannot act against the free will of those He desires to save. He honors the decisions of those who deliberately turn their backs on Him. This is the same danger Christ warns His disciples about in Matthew 10:17-22, noting that only those whose faith endures to the very end will be saved subjectively: "Be on your guard (*says Jesus*) against men; they will hand you over to the local councils and flog you in their synagogues. On my account you will be brought before governors and kings as witnesses to them and to the Gentiles. But when they arrest you, do not worry about what to say or how to say it. At that time you will be given what to say, for it will not be you speaking, but the Spirit of your Father speaking through you. Brother will betray brother to death, and a father his child; children will rebel against their parents and have them put to death. All men will hate you because of me, but he who stands firm to the end (*in other words, those whose faith endures to the end*) will be saved." Salvation is guaranteed only as long as believers hold onto their faith in Christ.

While faith has no saving virtue in and of itself, it is the means by which believers say to God, "Yes, I accept Your gift of salvation through Christ."

Turning back to Hebrews 6, we see this truth is clearly expressed in verses 4-6: "It is impossible for those who have once been enlightened (*that is, those who have understood the gospel*), who have tasted the heavenly gift (*the good news of salvation*), who have shared in the Holy Spirit (*experienced the new birth*), who have tasted the goodness of the word of God (*that is, the promise of eternal life*), and the powers of the coming age, if they fall away, to be brought back to repentance, because to their loss they are crucifying the Son of God all over again and subjecting him to public disgrace."

While believers may indeed remain nominal members of the family of God, they may at any time bid farewell to their faith and to the blessings offered in Christ. This is the warning Paul gives the believers in Hebrews 10:22 and onward. For this reason believers must encourage one another through good deeds and fellowship, especially as signs tell us that the Second Coming is at the door.

Meeting Together

To this end, Paul in Hebrews 10:25 encourages his readers: "Let us not give up meeting together, as some are in the habit of doing." In other words, do not stop attending church. Do not feel that you can continue being a strong Christian while remaining at home. The church is the body of Christ, and if you cut the hand from the body, that hand will wither away. If you cut a branch from the trunk or from the vine, you are removing it from the source of life.

Jesus says in John 15:4, "Abide in me, and I in you." Paul says in verse 25, "Let us not give up meeting together, as some are in the habit of doing, but let us encourage one another."

One purpose of corporate worship is to encourage other believers to hold onto their faith, especially as they face distress and persecution, "and all the more as you see the Day approaching." The word "Day" refers to the Lord's Second Coming, which the Bible says will be preceded by great tribulation.

Deliberate Disbelief

Verse 26 adds a sobering admonition, "If we deliberately keep on sinning after we have received the knowledge of the truth, no sacrifice for sins is left."

We must not interpret this verse out of context, as many are tempted to do. The "sin" Paul is referring to in verse 26 is not sin against the law, but the sin of unbelief. Any sin committed against the law is forgiven, because Jesus paid the price for every sin committed against the law. But when a believer sins against grace—which is the sin of unbelief—he or she is willfully rejecting the gift of salvation in Christ. And since God created human beings with free will, and since God is Love, He will not force salvation on those who deliberately reject the Savior, Jesus Christ.

Paul says in verse 26 that the only valid sacrifice that can forgive sins and qualify the believer for heaven is the sacrifice of Christ on the cross (in contrast to animal sacrifices). The animal sacrifices are a type, or symbol. They were offered continually and had no power to save.

But that one sacrifice of Jesus on the cross legally paid the price for the sins of the entire human race and is the only sacrifice that is acceptable before the law to forgive sins.

Those who reject that sacrifice willfully—knowingly—have no other sacrifice that can atone for the sin of unbelief in Jesus. Without faith in Jesus, a human being has no hope.

Verses 26-29 clearly underscore that Paul in this passage is talking exclusively about the sin of unbelief. Verses 26 and 27 say that "when there is a deliberate rejection of Christ, which is the sin of unbelief, then there is nothing else to face but a fearful expectation of judgment and of raging fire that will consume the enemies of God...." To reject Christ, as pointed out in Hebrews 6, is to crucify Christ afresh.

Only two options are open to the human family when dealing with Christ and Him crucified. They can either cry like the unbelievers of 2,000 years ago, "Crucify Him" or can choose to be crucified with Him. In Galatians 2:20 Paul shares the only truly Christian response: "I am crucified with Christ,"which means that one accepts the death of Christ as one's own death. Paul says in Romans 6 and verse 7 that those who have died to sin have been justified (freed) from sin.

Paul says in verse 27 that those who reject Christ deliberately, persistently, and ultimately have nothing to which to look forward except the judgment of God. Verse 28 says, "Anyone who rejected the law of Moses died without mercy on the testimony of two or three witnesses."

In Old Testament times, if a person broke the law of Moses and the act was witnessed by two or more persons, the sentence could be death. Verse 29 says: "How much more severely do you think a man deserves to be punished who has trampled the Son God under foot, who has treated as an unholy thing the blood of the covenant that sanctified him, and who has insulted the Spirit of grace."

A person who clearly understands and accepts the gospel has no excuse for turning deliberately from the gift of salvation. In doing so, they deliberately choose the curse of the law—eternal death.

Deliberate Disregard

Before Moses passed away, he spoke to the Israelites and basically said this, "God has placed before you a blessing and a curse, a life and death and God's will is that you choose that life, that blessing, that you and your children might live."

On the cross, Christ paid the price for the sins of the entire human race. God so loved the world (*the human race*) that He gave His only begotten Son.

In Romans 8:32 we find that God spared not His own Son; did not spare Him from the terrible agony of the death of the cross but delivered Him up for all mankind.

This proves that salvation has already been obtained in Christ for the entire human race, and, as John 3:16 says: "Whosoever believeth shall not perish but have everlasting life (KJV)."

Then John tells us in verse 17 that God did not send His Son into the world to condemn the world (which is what humanity deserves) but to save the world through Him. That is salvation through grace. That is the good news of the gospel.

But now comes verse 18: "Whoever believes in him is not condemned."

The moment a person believes in Christ, he or she passes from death to life. On the other hand, "but whoever does not believe stands condemned already because he has not believed in the name of God's one and only Son."

God does not condemn any of us for being sinners—after all, by nature we are born to sin. But God does condemn us when we deliberately, persistently, ultimately reject His gift of salvation in Christ. May none of us ever choose this pathway in our lives.

Serious Salvation

Before moving on, we need to couple the thoughts of verse 18 with those of John 3:36, which reads: "Whoever believes in the Son has eternal life, but whoever rejects the Son will not see life, for God's wrath remains on him."

No human being will be lost simply because he or she was born into sin. A person is lost only when he or she deliberately, persistently and ultimately rejects the gift of salvation in Christ. But this also applies to the believer who ultimately turns his back to Christ. Hebrews 10 delivers this message repeatedly.

Believers must never treat their salvation in Christ lightly. While salvation is a gift, they must never forget that God saved them at the cost of the cross. So God cannot simply forgive anyone who deliberately rejects the gift of salvation. As long as they are under the umbrella of justification by faith, the believers' salvation is guaranteed. Nobody can take it away from them, but when they turn their backs on Christ—when they give up their faith in Christ—then they deliberately are doing what the world did to Christ. They are deliberately crucifying Christ afresh. They are rejecting—turning their backs on—the only thing that can save them. This is why a believer's faith is the most valuable thing they have on earth. Some may believe that a credit card is an asset. Yet, bank accounts, real estate, and good credit—wonderful as these things are—cannot take a person to heaven. These are undoubtedly some of the most valuable things human beings claim as their own. But these can be destroyed—taken away. The believer's most valuable possession is not something tangible. It can be seen only with the eye of faith—and that is faith in Christ.

In Hebrews 10:35 the apostle Paul tells his readers not to throw away their confidence. Their faith will be richly rewarded, he assures them. They should not give up their faith in Christ.

Persevere to the End

Then in verse 36 Paul tells his readers to persevere so that when they have done God's will and endured to the end by faith, they will receive what He has promised. Why? "For in just a very little while, he who is coming will come and will not delay" (Hebrews 10:37).

In other words, "Keep your eyes focused on Christ until He comes the second time to take you home."

Verses 38 and 39 summarizes very clearly what Paul has been saying: "But my righteous one will live by faith" (KJV).

"The just shall live by faith,"Paul says in another English translation, though the text literally reads, "He that is just by faith shall live. And if he shrinks back, I will not be pleased with him."

In other words, Paul is saying, "If after you have accepted Christ as your righteousness—if after you come under the umbrella of justification by faith—you turn your back on this wonderful truth, God cannot save you against your own will. Yes, the gift is still there, but if you turn your back on the gift; if you say, 'I do not want it any more' for whatever reason, then God will not force you into heaven."

My prayer for us is found in verse 39, "But we are not of those who shrink back and are destroyed, but of those who believe and are saved."

The moment a person believes in Christ, they pass from death to life. The moment they believe and come under the umbrella of justification by faith they have peace with God. But if they shrink back from faith, they will lose the gift of salvation. In deliberately abandoning faith, the believer forfeits the blessed hope of eternal life and submits to be destroyed with all who reject Christ.

I pray that all believers reading this book will endure unto the end, so that one day we will be able to see each other physically and together rejoice in Christ and thank Him for the unspeakable gift of salvation.

CHAPTER 16
Hall of Faith
Hebrews 11:1-40

No chapter in Scripture deals with the subject of faith as eloquently as the 11th chapter of the book of Hebrews. Its placement here is by no means coincidental, given Paul's concern last study that his readers develop unshakeable faith in Jesus.

The primary purpose of the Epistle to the Hebrews, in fact, is to strengthen the faith of first-century Jewish believers who were facing trials and tribulations.

Christians today must demonstrate this same enduring faith, especially as they face the final crises of earth's history. Hebrews 11 most certainly applies to Christians in the 21st century—perhaps more so because, as the end approaches, things will get more and more difficult. The devil will do his best to separate the believers from their faith in Christ—Hebrews 11 is therefore extremely important to Christians today.

This chapter is often called the Hall of Faith, for here we see listed names of men and women who in spite of persecution, danger, distress, and hardship, held onto their faith in Christ to the very end. This chapter extols their amazing faith through time and experience.

Faith Defined

The first six verses of Hebrews 11 define faith. The writer then uses the rest of the chapter to show how faith works, as modeled by Old Testament saints. Since many Christians today rightly believe they are living in the very last days of world history at a time when their faith will be tested to the limit, Hebrews 11 is a chapter well worth studying.

Appropriately enough we begin this study by considering what faith is *not*, for many have false concepts about faith. One of the first things we learn is that faith *is not* simply "positive thinking". If faith were simply "positive thinking" (as some evangelists preach), faith would be a subtle form of works.

Second, faith *is not* a "hunch" to follow to the kingdom, though some nominal Christians seem to have this philosophy about faith. And third, faith *is not* some sixth sense Christians feel inside themselves.

What then *is* faith, if not positive thinking, a hunch, or an inner light? Some hold that to have faith is to believe that everything will come out okay in the end. But this is not faith. Faith, in fact, has no basis in feelings, though faith *affects* feelings.

At times everything seems to go well for Christians, and their faith and their feelings are as one. But when they face persecution, distress, famine, or need, sometimes their faith and their feelings part company. Which leads to the fourth definition of what faith *is not*: Faith *is not* believing that all is well. And finally, having faith is not a make-believe experience.

If faith is not these five things—positive thinking, a hunch to be followed, an inner light, feeling that all is well, and making believe, what then *is* faith?

Hebrews' Definition

Hebrews 11 in its very first verse defines faith: "Faith is being sure of what we hope for and certain of what we do not see." Faith means being *absolutely sure* of what one hopes for and *absolutely certain* of what one does not physically see. Faith is the substance of reality, of things a Christian is absolutely sure of, though they may not possess them at the moment. What are these as-yet-unclaimed realities?

The first is the righteousness of Christ. Faithful Christians are absolutely sure that one day they will be made righteous. Romans 5:19 brings this out. "By one Man's obedience the many (*the believers*) will be constituted righteous" (Amplified Bible).

The second certainty of faith is that of eternal life, for Jesus says in John 5:24: "He who believes in the Father who sent me and he who believes in me, has everlasting life and has already passed from death to life" (NKJV).

The third certainty is the absolute assurance of heaven. Jesus says in John 14:1-3: "Do not let your hearts be troubled. You believe in me, believe in God. I go to heaven to prepare a place for you and I will come again and take you where I am."

Of these three things true faith is absolutely certain: of righteousness, of eternal life, and of living someday with the Lord. At the moment the believer has none of these. Christians are not yet righteous—Martin Luther puts it well when he points out that all believers are simultaneously sinners and righteous. They are sinners in and of themselves but righteous in Christ. Faith is sure of this. They are absolutely guaranteed righteousness in Christ, though their feelings may ebb and flow.

Faith and Dissatisfaction

Having faith in a better future implies that Christians are dissatisfied with their present reality. Note Hebrews 11:8-10: "By faith Abraham, when called to go to a place he would later receive as his inheritance, obeyed and went, even though he did not know where he was going. By faith he made his home in the promised land like a stranger in a foreign country; he lived in tents, as did Isaac and Jacob, who were heirs with him of the same promise. For he was looking forward to the city with foundations, whose architect and builder is God."

To have faith is to have absolute assurance of righteousness to come, eternal life, and heaven—though none are yet in hand. What Christians have today is sin, death, and life on earth. They are still living in enemy territory.

Faith and Science

Besides these three elements, true faith always has a focus—an object—and the object of true faith is *never* the Christian's performance. It is not their opinions that count but what Jesus Christ did as the Word of God made flesh.

Faith takes God at His word, though worldly wisdom and the scientific method may disagree. Hebrews 11:3 says: "By faith we understand that the universe was formed at God's command, so that what is seen was not made out of what was visible."

Science today wrestles with the conundrum of how matter came to be in the universe, but God was not dependent on pre-existing matter to create the world. His breath and His word are energy and power. He spoke and it happened. This transcends human rationale and the scientific method. Far too many Christians now accept evolution as a probability.

But no, we do not come from monkeys. This earth was not developed through millions of years of progression. Our magnificent world, though ruined by sin, did not come into existence by chance but by the Word of God. We can't prove scientifically what Genesis 1 describes about creation, but we know one thing—having faith means taking God at His Word. And I believe that if we reject this wonderful truth, we are in trouble. God did not depend on pre-existing matter as evolutionists do. He spoke and it happened. If we cannot accept this, what do we do with the assertion that when Christ comes the second time He will shout with the voice of the archangel and many in their graves will be raised?

How can we believe that Christ can raise the dead with a shout—bodies disintegrated by thousands of years of time—if we reject His creative power? If we deny the Genesis record of creation, we must deny the blessed hope of the resurrection, or perhaps interpret the resurrection as something that will take millions of years to materialize. This is not what the Bible teaches.

Hebrews 11:3 says clearly: "By faith we understand that the universe was formed at God's command." He spoke and it happened. We can't prove it. We can't rationalize it, but we believe it because God's Word says so. Faith is taking God at His Word. Faith is saying, "Not I, but Christ." It is such faith that qualified Abel to be righteous in the eyes of God. It is such faith that qualified Enoch to go to heaven. In other words, without faith it is impossible to please God, for when we come to God in faith we are really saying, "Not I, but Christ."

Hebrews 11:4-6 says: "By faith Abel offered God a better sacrifice than Cain did. By faith he was commended as a righteous man, when God spoke well of his offerings. And by faith he still speaks even though he is dead. By faith Enoch was taken from this life, so that he did not experience death; he could not be found, because God had taken him away. For before he was taken, he was commended as one who pleased God (*remember, we please God by faith alone*). And without faith it is impossible to please God, because anyone who comes to him must believe that he exists and that he rewards those who earnestly seek him."

Three Elements of Faith

In light of what the first six verses of Hebrews 11 say about faith, we find that true faith contains three elements: First, faith knows God's

Word and His gift of salvation in Christ. Romans 10:17 says: "Faith comes from hearing the message, and the message is heard through the word of Christ." Jesus Himself says in John 8:32: "You will know the truth, and the truth will set you free." By the word "truth". He means Himself, for He brings out in John 8:36: "If the Son sets you free, you shall be free indeed." Genuine faith begins with knowledge of the truth as it is in Christ.

But it is not enough simply to *know* the truth. The second element of faith is that one must *believe*—one must believe God when He says that Christ has already redeemed His people; that as Ephesians 2:6 says, "we are already sitting in heavenly places in Christ."

The Bible says many things that lie beyond human comprehension. It tells us, for example, that God put humanity into Christ to qualify Him to save the world.

Now, *how* could God put humanity *into* Christ some 2,000 years ago? we rationally ask. How could God put us in Christ before we were born? When Jesus told Nicodemus, "You must be born again,"his rational mind rebelled. He was an old man! How could he enter his mother's womb and be born again? But faith takes God at His Word. Faith says, "Yes, God, I believe that you put me into Christ 2,000 years ago. I believe that you rewrote my history. I believe that you changed my status from condemnation to justification. I believe all these things, not because it makes sense to me or because scientists can prove it, but because Your Word says so." The measuring stick of all eternal truth is the Bible, the Word of God.

The third element of true faith is obedience. The faithful Christian surrenders his or her will to the truth as it is in Christ, no matter what science or others say. To have faith is to obey the Word of God. Faith is saying, "Yes, God. I accept the life of Christ as my life. I accept His death as my death. I accept His resurrection as my resurrection. I accept His ascension as my ascension. I accept His sitting at the right hand of the father as mine. In other words, I accept the holy history of Christ as my history." Faith surrenders the will to the truth as it is in Christ.

Crucified with Christ

The moment believers do this, they join Paul in proclaiming in principle the words of Galatians 2:20: "I have been crucified with

Christ and I no longer live, but Christ lives in me." Faith believes the impossible. Faith believes in the supernatural. Faith believes in the truth as it is in Christ.

Hall of Faith

Hebrews 11:7-40 needs little explanation, for it consists largely of a list of men and women who have the kind of faith described in the first six verses of the chapter. These men and women—this "Hall of Faith"—based their faith on the Word of God and believed in the promised Messiah and faithfully obeyed the truth as it is in Christ.

We would be doing Paul and this eloquent passage a deep injustice, however, were we to ignore six main points that emerge. The first point is that *faith is capable of believing the impossible*—the supernatural. For example, Noah believes the flood will come, though it has never rained before. In verse 7 Sarah believes God will give her a son, though she has passed the age of childbearing.

In verses 11 and 12 Abraham believes God will raise Isaac to life after he has been sacrificed, for God always keeps His promises (verse 19). Faith takes God at His Word, regardless of scientific improbabilities.

Point two is that faith is sure about the ultimate future. This point comes up in verses 8-10, where Abraham, Isaac, and Jacob—the fathers of Israel—know they will ultimately reach heaven, so they do not mind living in tents in their present life because of their hope in the future. Jesus Himself says of Abraham, "Abraham saw My day and rejoiced."

The third attribute of faith revealed in this "Hall of Faith" is that faith acts on the basis of God's revealed Word. This is what some refer to as "faith in action,"or as the New Testament puts it, "works of faith". The Hebrews 11 heroes all act according to the promises and directions God shares with them. Noah faithfully builds the ark; Abraham leaves home without knowing for sure where he will end up; Abraham prepares willingly to offer up Isaac, his son; Moses' faith leads him to refuse the pleasures of sin for a season.

And the list goes on in Hebrews 11, as men and women act on God's revealed Word. To them, faith is reality in Christ.

The fourth attribute of those worthy of this "Hall of Faith" is that they are certain of God's promise. Verses 23-26 tell us that Moses' faith in the future motivated his behavior in Egypt. He was willing to suffer with God's people rather than enjoy the pleasures of Egypt for a season.

This lesson is important to those today who are looking forward to the Second Coming of Christ, for materialism can draw believers out of Christ. Paul writes in 1 Timothy 6:10: "The love of money is the root of all kinds of evil. Some people, eager for money, have wandered from the faith."

The fifth characteristic of the supremely faithful listed in Hebrews 11 is that they ignore evidence contrary to God's Word. The scientific world often seems to contradict the Word of God. Science believes that there can be no resurrection of the dead—that death is the end. Science teaches that human beings cannot travel through the universe without oxygen masks. Science disbelieves many things promised in the Bible. But faith ignores anything that contradicts the Word of God. Though the faithful may be unable to explain the science behind what they believe, they elect to believe the Word of God. Noah had no scientific evidence that it would, or could rain, yet he believed God. Abraham believed that his wife would give birth to a son, thought she had passed the age of childbearing.

And finally—this is the ultimate purpose of this chapter and the whole book of Hebrews—faith never gives up, even against mounting odds (verses 13 and 37 to 39).

A Time of Tribulation

All the heroes of Hebrews 11 had one thing in common. Their faith endured to the end because they were absolutely sure of God's Word. These men and women of the Old Testament died without having seen the acts of Christ. But they died with hope, secure that God's promise would be fulfilled.

We who are living in New Testament times have even greater reason to believe, for Christ is more than a promise—He is reality. He was born and lived in this world, died on the cross, was resurrected, and ascended into heaven.

Should not our faith be even stronger than the faith of those Old

Testament giants of faith? The Bible clearly teaches that a time of trouble—a great tribulation—will soon test the faith of all believers. While faithful Christians will not experience the full force of the seven last plagues, their faith will be severely tested, and only those with unshakeable faith will be able to stand.

Revelation 6:12-17 describes the signs of the Second Coming. Verse 15 seems to imply that perhaps nobody will be able to stand when He comes in His glory the second time. Chief priests, captains, masters, and slaves all seem unable to stand. John asks at the end of Revelation 6, "Who shall be able to stand?"

Revelation 7 answers the question. There we find God holding the winds of strife until His people are sealed. The believers' faith needs to be sealed as they face the end time. Their faith needs to become unshakeable.

I pray that the faith of all believers will remain constantly focused on Jesus Christ, the Author and Finisher of their salvation.

CHAPTER 17

Christ—The Supreme Example
Hebrews 12:1-4

As he has done from the beginning of the book, the writer of Hebrews in Chapter 12 continues his quest to strengthen the faith of his readers.

In the first four verses he presents Christ as the Christian's supreme Example and Source of faith. But before we look at these important verses, let us set the stage by reviewing how heroes of the Old Testament manifested faith, as recorded in Hebrews 11's "Hall of Faith".

Manifestations of Faith

We found last chapter that faith takes God at His Word and believes even that which seems impossible or supernatural. Faithful men and women listed in Hebrews 11 take God at His Word, even though it may contradict prevailing medical, scientific, and social wisdom of the times.

A second trait of these heroic figures of faith is that they are absolutely confident of future glory. Despite hardship and danger, they have absolute confidence in God's promises.

Their third trait is that these heroes of faith take action based on their faith. The hope of glory motivates Christians even today, as assuredly as it did in Old Testament times.

These faithful heroes' fourth characteristic is that they live in the future. While most human beings concentrate on the present, people who walk by faith know that this present life is only temporary. They live in the future because they are looking forward to a life to come.

A fifth characteristic of the heroicly faithful is that they are not affected by public opinion or peer pressure. They know in whom they believe and know that He is faithful in what He promises. Their faith is unshakeable in the Word of God.

The final characteristic we noted last chapter is that these faithful ones persevere to the end because they believe their ultimate salvation is worth everything—even life itself.

A Cloud of Witnesses

The history of these Old Testament heroes of Hebrews 11 all illustrate the qualities of faith that inspire Christians of all times to remain true to Jesus Christ. And in the radiance of their examples we begin our study of Hebrews 12:1: "Therefore, since we are surrounded by such a great cloud of witnesses, (*referring to the men and women whose names Paul recorded in Hebrews 11*) let us throw off everything that hinders and the sin that so easily entangles, and let us run with perseverance the race marked out for us."

Because of the constant danger of giving up the faith, especially in the coming end-time crisis, Christians today should throw away every negative thing (*sin*) that may cause them to give up their faith in Christ.

The devil constantly tries to destroy the Christian's faith. As we studied last chapter, the righteousness that qualifies a person for heaven, now and in the judgment, is always in Christ. The Lord is in heaven today, where no thief can steal it away. But the faith that makes that righteousness effective in His followers resides in them. Christians live in a sinful world still affected by Satan's control, and the Evil One will do his utmost to destroy faith in Jesus Christ.

He tries persecution, perversion of the gospel, and materialism to pull the believers out of Christ. The writer of Hebrews is basically saying, "Let us allow none of these things to weaken or destroy our faith, as we look to Old Testament heroes of faith as our examples."

Running the Race

Paul then goes on to challenge us with these words, "Let us run with perseverance the race marked out for us." Two things jump out from Paul's writings on this issue. The first is that whenever Paul talks about salvation as a gift, he says it comes *only* by faith. But whenever he talks about Christian living after conversion, he compares it to a *race*.

Paul knew that in the Olympic races, the one purpose in participating was to *come in first*. But in the Christian life, he says, believers enter the race, not to come first, but to finish the course. In God's race, everyone who finishes the course wins. Jesus says in Matthew 10:22: "He who endures (*or perseveres*) to the end will be saved" (NKJV).

Christians must not give up the race midway. This is the whole point of the book of Hebrews. So once again he brings it forward in Hebrews 12:1.

He presses on in verses 2 and 3, presenting Jesus Christ as the Christians' greatest example: "Let us fix our eyes on Jesus, the author and perfecter of our faith, who for the joy set before him endured the cross, scorning its shame, and sat down at the right hand of the throne of God. Consider him who endured such opposition from sinful men, so that you will not grow weary and lose heart."

Lack of Appreciation

During the 1960s, 1970s, and 1980s, my wife and I had the privilege of spending 18 years in mission service in East Africa. In the early days of mission work in Africa, missionaries would face extreme hardships. Life was hard and transportation difficult.

But times changed. Many if not most physical hardships of mission service have been resolved. But in today's world, with its strong emphasis on independence and self sufficiency, missionaries are often not appreciated in foreign lands. Many missionaries today give up their mission posts, not because of physical hardships but because they sense no appreciation from those they try to serve.

When Jesus appeared on earth as a missionary from heaven, He too received litte appreciation. Even His disciples forsook Him at the cross. Jesus was mistreated; He was abused; He was falsely accused, and at last crucified on the cruel Roman cross. But He endured all these things unto the very end. Why? Because of the joy that was set before Him of saving humanity.

God loved the world so much that He was willing to give His Son so whoever believes in Him should not perish. God was willing to be in Christ reconciling the world to Himself. Christ was willing to give up His wonderful, lofty position as the Son of God, as the second Person of the Godhead. He gave up all His divine prerogatives, joined Himself to the human race that needed redeeming, and became a slave (Philippians 2:6).

We are told that Jesus was equal with God and that it was not robbery for Him to be equal with God. He emptied Himself, made Himself of no reputation, became a slave, and was made in the likeness of men before going to his death on the cross. Christ endured hardship, abuse, mistreatment and finally crucifixion that humanity might have a place in heaven.

John 13:1 brings this out clearly: "It was just before the Passover feast. Jesus knew that the time had come for Him to leave this world and go to the Father. Having loved his own who were in the world, he now showed them the full extent of His love (*He loved us to the very end* [KJV])."

He did not give up on His earthly mission. The writer of Hebrews says that His followers, for the joy of glorifying their Savior, must also endure unto the end, though it may cause them their lives.

Jesus said not to fear those who kill the body but those who can destroy the soul. They must not give up their faith in Christ, no matter what happens (Matthew 10:28).

Notice that for the believers' faith to endure unto the end, their eyes must be fixed on Jesus, the Author and Finisher of their faith. Salvation from beginning to end is only through faith in Christ. The apostle Paul puts it this way in Romans 1:17: "Salvation is by faith from first to last."

From beginning to end, salvation takes place through faith. Whether in one's standing before God (justification by faith) or Christian living (fruits of salvation), all is accomplished through faith.

Faithful to Death

Having encouraged his readers to hold onto their faith to the very end, Paul then reminds them that they have not yet struggled against sin to the point of shedding blood—that is, dying for their faith as the heroes of the Old Testament and Christ Himself did. In Hebrews 12:4 Paul says: "In your struggle against sin, you have not yet resisted to the point of shedding your blood."

This, of course, is true of most Christians today. Christians living today may indeed be called upon to die for their faith, but Paul is writing to living Christians who have not yet made that sacrifice. By "sin" in this passage and elsewhere in the chapter, Paul is primarily referring to the sin of unbelief. When he says, "Let us run the race with perseverance, let us fix our eyes on our Lord Jesus Christ, the Author and Finisher of our faith, let us throw off everything that hinders and the sin that so easily besets us. . . .", the sin in question is not sinning against the law but sinning against the gospel—against grace.

This was a danger to the early Jewish Christians and a grave danger to Christians today. Every sin against the law can be forgiven, for Christ's blood was shed for the forgiveness of sins against the law. But because God created humanity with free will, He cannot forgive those who deliberately reject the gift of salvation and commit the sin of unbelief.

If anyone deliberately keeps on rejecting Jesus Christ after receiving the true knowledge of the gospel, he is rejecting the only sacrifice that can cancel or forgive sin. Those who deliberately reject the Spirit of grace are deliberately trampling the Son of God under foot and have no further recourse (Hebrews 10:26).

In John 16:8-11 Jesus explains the mission of the Holy Spirit—an assignment never to be confused with the work of Christ. Christ physically came to earthy 2,000 years ago to save mankind—that was His work. The Holy Spirit is not a co-Redeemer with Christ but a Communicator of the gospel. He is the third Person of the Godhead whose mission is to lead humanity into all truth and communicate the salvation that Christ has already obtained. In John 16:8 Jesus says that the Holy Spirit will convict the world of three things: of sin, of righteousness, and of judgment.

In the following three verses (9-11) Jesus explains each of them. Notice in verse 9 that sin is defined by Jesus as unbelief: "In regard to sin, because men do not believe in me."

In other words, it does not matter how good a person is or how much he or she has accomplished as an individual. If a person is without Christ, he or she is lost. The Bible says it is impossible for men and women to save themselves through their own good works. Salvation is by grace alone, and that grace is by faith in Jesus Christ. One who rejects Christ is committing the sin of unbelief—the unpardonable sin.

In verse 10, then, Christ explains righteousness, noting that He is going to the Father after fulfilling His mission. While Jesus has been on earth, the Father has been Chairman of salvation. On the cross Jesus cried, "It is finished." When He rose from the dead and Mary, who was the first to see him that resurrection morning, took hold of his ankle, Jesus told her that she should not cling to Him "because I have not yet gone to My Father and your Father and to My God and to your God."

After he returns from presenting Himself to the Father, He tells the disciples in Matthew 28:18, "All authority in heaven and on earth has been given to me. Therefore go and make disciples of nations, baptizing them in the name of the Father and of the Son and of the Holy Spirit."

Jesus' going to heaven simply points to the fact that the salvation He obtained in His earthly mission was absolutely perfect and complete. No one can add anything to it and no one can improve on it. It must simply be accepted by faith.

If a person knows this truth and deliberately rejects it, there is nothing left for him or her but the judgment. Man is not lost because he is a sinner (John 3:18, 36). God does not blame us for something for which we are not responsible. God does not blame us for being born with a sinful nature, but God will blame those who deliberately and ultimately reject Jesus Christ as Savior. This is because salvation is a gift and there is no excuse for rejecting it.

Children of Three Fathers

In concluding these four verses on the importance of an enduring faith, we note how God gave the Jewish nation three fathers, Abraham, Isaac, and Jacob. Throughout the Old Testament and even in the New Testament, these three men together are used to represent the living. Jesus said to the Sadducees on one occasion, "God is not a God of the dead; He is the God of the living,"as in, "the God of Abraham, Isaac, and Jacob" (Matthew 22:31 and 32).

Why these three men? Because the three basic character elements they possess must also belong to every believer—every child of life.

Romans 4 and Galatians 3 tell us what these characteristics are. Abraham stands for faith. This is the starting point for new believers in their subjective experiences.

Romans 4:16-18 says: "Therefore, the promise comes by faith (*that is, the promise of salvation*), so that it may be by grace and may be guaranteed to all Abraham's offspring—not only to those who are of the law (*that is, the Jews*) but also to those who are of the faith of Abraham. He is the father of us all. As it is written: 'I have made you a father (*that is, a prototype*) of many nations.'" Abraham is the father of all Christians in the sight of God—the God who gives life to the dead and calls things that are not as though they were. Against all hope, Abraham in hope believed and so became the father of many nations, just as God had told him, "So shall your offspring be." To be a child of Abraham, one need not have the blood of Abraham but one must have Abraham's faith.

Isaac's Role

Isaac is the second father portrayed in the Old Testament. What is so special about him? The Old Testament seems to indicate that Isaac accomplished little of note, compared to his father Abraham. But what *is* special is Isaac's birth. He was born at a time when it was scientifically impossible for his mother, Sarah, to bear a child. Where Abraham stands for *faith*, Isaac stands for *new birth*—being born from above as the Holy Spirit is invited into a Christian's being. Jesus once told a Jewish leader named Nicodemus that "Unless you are born from above, unless you are born of the Spirit, you cannot enter into the kingdom of God (John 3:3 NKJV) .

A new Christian must not only believe but experience a new birth through the power of the indwelling Holy Spirit. After all, even the devil believes—in terms of mental assent. This new-birth experience is illustrated by the life of Isaac (See Galatians 4:28).

Jacob Who Persevered

Finally there is Jacob, son of Isaac, whose name means "schemer". God had promised Jacob's mother, Rebecca, that though Jacob was younger than his brother Esau, Jacob would receive the birthright commonly given to the oldest son. True to his name "Schemer", Jacob tried his best through life to defraud Esau of his birthright by manipulation and trickery.

Finally Jacob, now an old man, gave up his scheming ways during an all-night wrestling match with a stranger—a stranger who turned out to be an angel. Jacob could not subdue the stranger, and as dawn approached the angel dislocated Jacob's hip, effectively ending the match. But though in excruciating pain, Jacob refused to let go of the angel. "I will not let you go until you bless me,"he cried out.

The angel replied with a question, "What is your name?"

Jacob told him, and the angel replied, "No longer. From now on you shall be called Israel, which means a person who has prevailed."

Jacob stands for faith that endures to the end.

The Believers' Needs

Believers who possess the faith of Abraham will believe that Jesus Christ is the Messiah, the Savior of the world. Through heart-obedience they will experience the new birth through the indwelling Holy Spirit, as represented by Isaac, for unless they experience that new birth, they cannot enter the kingdom of heaven. And finally, most important of all, like Jacob they must persevere. Yes, they will face hardships. They will face distress, famine, nakedness, and all kinds of problems. But they must never, never give up their faith.

CHAPTER 18

God's Refining Process
Hebrews 12:5-11

Paul expresses great concern in Hebrews 12:1-4 (last chapter's passage) about the spiritual endurance of Jewish converts to Christianity who may be losing their faith and salvation in Christ. Christian living is a battle and a march, he says, and the devil works constantly to challenge and destroy faith in Jesus. But by the grace of God, faith can endure to the end.

With this background in mind, we move to Hebrews 12:5-11, which focuses on God's refining process for His people.

When by the power of the Holy Spirit people respond to the gospel message, they repent and by faith receive Jesus Christ as their personal Savior. A radical change takes place in their minds and attitudes, but no change occurs in their sinful nature.

Paradox of Sin

Sin, then, becomes a paradox for the Christian. The converted mind, on the one hand, bids farewell to sin—it has died to sin, as Romans 6:2 puts it. But the unconverted (and unconvertible) flesh remains enslaved to sin. The converted mind, now under the direction of the indwelling Spirit, wants to do the will of God. But the flesh opposes this will. So Christian living becomes a battle between the Spirit, who wants to control the converted mind, and the flesh controlled by Satan.

Paul brings this out forcefully in Galatians 5:16-18: "So I say, live by the Spirit, and you will not gratify the desires of the sinful nature. For the sinful nature desires what is contrary to the Spirit, and the Spirit what is contrary to the sinful nature. They are in conflict with each other, so that you do not do what you want. But if you are led by the Spirit you are not under the law."

To be under the law means to be under its jurisdiction, and the law says: "Obey and you can live. If you disobey you will die."

Those under the law must produce that obedience. But those walking in the Spirit are under grace and are depending entirely on Christ's righteousness to save them.

Even those depending entirely on the Spirit in their Christian living, however, find that Christian living is a struggle. Their salvation in Christ is secure as long as they remain under the umbrella of justification by faith. Of this they can be absolutely sure. But their Christian walk is not as smooth as their security in Christ. Their Christian walk is always a battle, a constant struggle between the desires of the converted mind and the pull of the sinful nature, which wants its selfish way. This inner turmoil is graphically described in Romans 7:15-24, a familiar passage.

But before we read it, we must remind ourselves that this passage is not talking about Paul's *pre-converted* experience. Clearly Paul is referring to Christians who have accepted Christ as their personal Savior and uses the generic "I" pronoun in reference to them. These are Christians who hate to do wrong and earnestly want to do the will of God, though in their performance they fall short of the goal. This is not at all the attitude of an unconverted person.

On the other hand, the passage makes no mention of the power of the Holy Spirit. What we have in the passage, then, is a genuine Christian who wants to serve God and is trying to do so by his or her own strength.

Those who try to do this always end up frustrated, and in the very next chapter, Romans 8, Paul says that by walking in the Spirit, Christians no longer need to gratify the sinful desires of their flesh.

Christian living, even so, is always a struggle, Paul says, for the flesh constantly tries to lift its ugly head and demand what it wants.

A Slave to Sin

Paul describes this struggle dramatically in Romans 7:14: "We know that the law is spiritual; but I am unspiritual, sold as a slave to sin." Paul is talking here about his sinful nature, as he continues in verses 15-18: "I do not understand what I do. For what I want to do I do not do, but what I hate I do. And if I do what I do not want to do, I agree that the law is good. As it is, it is no longer I myself who do it (*that is, the converted mind*), but it is sin living in me. I know that nothing good lives in me, that is, in my sinful nature. For I have the desire to do what is good (*that is, my mind desires to what is good because it is converted*), but I cannot carry it out."

Verses 19-23 continue expressing the Christian's dilemma: "For what I do is not the good I want to do; no, the evil I do not want to do—this I keep on doing. Now if I do what I do not want to do, it is no longer I who do it, but it is sin living in me that does it. So I find this law (*this principle*) at work: When I want to do good, evil is right there with me. For in my inner being (*the converted mind*) I delight in God's law; but I see another law at work in the members of my body, waging war against the law of my mind and making me a prisoner of the law of sin at work within my members."

Paul ends this passage with a cry of anguish in verse 24: "What a wretched man I am! Who will rescue me from this body of death?" Paul is not asking "Who will save me?" This question has already been answered. Paul is crying for deliverance from the power of his flesh. The answer to his cry is found in Romans 7:25, where he says, "I thank God, through Jesus Christ," after finding relief through the work of the Holy Spirit, described in Romans 8.

Divine Refinement

Obtaining victory over the flesh is a painful process that Hebrews 12:5-11 defines in detail. Just as polishing a diamond involves removing rough edges, so refining Christians is a laborious process.

The Holy Spirit's primary purpose in the life of the believer is to reproduce the righteous life of Christ in them—not in order to save them (that is already accomplished), but so they can better witness for Christ. This process of sanctification, or holy living, involves subduing the sinful desires of the flesh and reproducing the righteousness of Christ. This dual process (reproducing the holy life of Christ while overcoming the flesh) is what Christian growth is all about.

Those as yet unfamiliar with this process may become very discouraged as the devil uses the struggle to try to pry the Christian out of Christ. "You might as well give up being a Christian, since you will never make it to heaven," he tells the struggling believer.

A Dangerous Measurement

Christians must never give in to the devil's temptation that they measure their performance as an indicator of whether or not they will be saved. Their eyes must remain fixed on Jesus Christ, the Author and Finisher of their faith. Paul has just told us in Hebrews 12:1-4 that above all else our faith must endure.

As mentioned at the beginning of this chapter, the main reason Paul writes this Epistle to the Hebrews is the danger that Jewish Christians of his day may give up their faith in Christ and return to Judaism. These Jewish Christians faced tremendous persecution from their families. When a Jew became a Christian, in fact, the parents would often hold a funeral service to show that their child was now the same as dead.

Paul writes this epistle to encourage them never to give up their faith in Christ, no matter how painful God's refining process. This is our focus in this chapter.

A Dual Process

The first thing we need to understand is that during sanctification, two processes take place at the same time. On the one hand, Christians must submit their sinful natures daily to the cross. On the other, the Holy Spirit is producing the life of Christ in them. This is the gospel formula for spiritual growth. Whether in justification by faith or sanctification by faith, the formula is always "Not I, but Christ," a negative and a positive.

This dual process is clearly taught throughout Scripture, so let us read some examples. We look first at Luke 9:23, where Jesus tells His disciples: "If anyone would come after me, he must deny himself (*the negative*) and take up his cross daily and follow me (*the positive*)."

In 2 Corinthians 4:10 Paul writes: "We always carry around us in our body the death of Jesus (*death to sin*), so that the life of Jesus may also be revealed in our body."

The manifestation of Christ in Christians' lives is seen in direct proportion to how much they have surrendered to the cross of Christ. The more they die to self, the more the Holy Spirit can reproduce in them the character of Christ.

Continuing in 2 Corinthians 4, we read in verse 11: "For we who are alive are always being given over to death for Jesus' sake, so that his life may be revealed in our mortal body."

Being put to death is a painful process, just as crucifixion was painful for Christ. Paul says in Galatians 5:24, in context of the fruit of the Spirit, "Those who belong to Christ Jesus have crucified the sinful nature with its passions and desires."

In Philippians 3:7-10 Paul says, "I give up all my self-righteousness. I deny all that I attain that I may win Christ and be found in Him not having my righteousness which is of the law but the righteousness that comes by faith."

Giving up one's own self-righteousness and putting up with hardship, Paul says, is painful but should not discourage the Christian. He reminds his readers that God's refining process is always done in love.

Growth Through Discipline

Returning to Hebrews 12:5 and 6, we read: "And you have forgotten that word of encouragement that addresses you as sons: 'My son, do not make light of the Lord's discipline, and do not lose heart when he rebukes you, because the Lord disciplines those he loves, and he punishes everyone he accepts as a son.'"

God's refining process is not punishment for sin or a rebuke for wrongdoing. We discover in verses 7 and 8 that enduring these hardships and divine disciplines is part of the Christian's growing-up process: "Endure hardship as discipline; God is treating you as sons. For what son is not disciplined by his father? If you are not disciplined (*everyone undergoes discipline*), then you are an illegitimate child and not true sons."

In the good old days, parents disciplined their children so they would grow up to be good, obedient citizens. But times have changed somewhat, and as one Englishman recently said, in the Western world, we know how to give our children everything but discipline.

I have discovered through ministering to prisoners that one reason many young men commit terrible crimes is that while they were growing up, they were thrown from one home to another and did not experience genuine love or discipline and never learned to discipline themselves.

Discipline begins on the outside so it can develop on the inside. God disciplines his followers for their own good. The flesh must be crucified if Christ is to be manifested.

Hebrews 12:9 and 10 continues Paul's discussion of discipline: "Moreover, we have all had human fathers who disciplined us and we respected them for it. How much more should we submit to the Father of our spirits and live! Our fathers disciplined us for a little while as they thought best; but God disciplines us for our good, that we may share in his holiness."

Christians must continually remind themselves that God's refining process, no matter how painful at the time, has as its only goal to reproduce the divine life of Christ. Christ Himself went through this process on earth. He endured it all, not for His own good, but for our salvation.

Made Perfect in Suffering

We are reminded of this in Hebrews 5:7: "During the days of Jesus' life on earth, he offered up prayers and petitions with loud cries and tears to the one who could save him from death, and he was heard because of his reverent submission."

Faith leads to reverent submission to God. In verses 8 and 9 Paul continues: "Although he was a son (*that is, the Son of God*), he learned obedience from what he suffered and, once made perfect, he became the source of eternal salvation for all who obey him and was designated by God to be high priest in the order of Melchizedek."

Christ, the Author of salvation, was made perfect by suffering. He denied His flesh so the Spirit could live in Him. In the Garden of Gethsemane, just hours before His death, Jesus prays, "Father, if it is possible, remove this cup."

The answer comes back, "No, Son. If I remove the cup, the world will be lost." Jesus responds, "Not My will but Thine be done."

God's whole purpose in the refining process is that believers in His Son should experience the righteousness of His Son. Only in this way can God convince the world that the gospel is not a theory, but the power of God unto salvation. When God refines us through His discipline, we must learn to count it all joy.

Unpleasant But Edifying

We now read Hebrews 12:11, which spells out the ultimate fruit of God's refining grace: "No discipline seems pleasant at the time." How true! Discipline can be painful. But when it later produces a harvest of righteousness and peace, what a joy!

Throughout Scripture we find statements about God's refining process. It's a vital process, if this earth is to be lightened with Christ's glory before the end of time. We live in a scientific age that will not accept anything that cannot be demonstrated.

The world has a crying need to see in Christianity a powerful demonstration of the life of Christ. A perceptive commentator on our times has noted that the trouble with the Christian church today is that it has substituted cultural Christianity for biblical Christianity.

Perhaps this is why there is often so little distinction between the carnal person of the world and Christians living carnal lives. If Christians truly want Christ's life to shine through them, they must be willing to be refined by the disciplinary process of their Lord, Jesus Christ.

The Bible is full of texts about spiritual discipline, and I recommend the following Old Testament passages: Deuteronomy 8:5, Job 5:17, Psalm 94:11-15, Proverbs 3:11, 12, Isaiah 48:10, and Malachi 3:1-3.

In the New Testament, for further study I recommend John 15:2, Romans 5:3-5, 2 Corinthians 4:15-18, and 1 Peter 1:3-7 and 4:12-14. End your study with Revelation 3:17-19.

These texts show convincingly that God's refining process is very much part and parcel of His redeeming grace. Among pagan faiths, outward spiritual refining is seen as a qualifier for salvation. But not so in Christianity. This refining process is designed to help the already saved Christian better manifest the life of Christ to others. To witness well for Christ, a believer must be willing to endure hardships and surmount obstacles as he or she submits to the Lord's discipline.

We close this chapter with Paul's encouraging words in Hebrews 12: 12,13: "Therefore, strengthen your feeble arms and weak knees. Make level paths for your feet, so that the lame may not be disabled, but rather healed."

CHAPTER 19

Living Under the New Covenant
Hebrews 12:12-29

The refining work of God in the life of believers drew our attention in the last chapter, as we studied Hebrews 12:5-11. We saw that during sanctification, life of the flesh is subdued so that life of the Spirit may be revealed to all.

Now in Hebrews 12:12-29 Paul examines the practical results of God's refining process under the New Covenant, as believers yield daily to the Spirit.

In the Old Covenant system—that is, under the law—the rules said "Obey and you will live. If you disobey, you will die." Living under that covenant was to live in constant fear of inevitable failures.

Under the New Covenant, however, Jesus says, "Abide in Me, and I in you for without Me you can do nothing (John 14)."

This new way of life has important practical results. Hebrews 12: 12- 17 points us to three of those results. The passage reads: "Therefore, strengthen your feeble arms and weak knees. Make level paths for your feet, so that the lame may not be disabled, but rather healed. Make every effort to live in peace with all men and to be holy; without holiness no one will see the Lord. See to it that no one misses the grace of God and that no bitter root grows up to cause trouble and defile many. See that no one is sexually immoral, or is godless like Esau, who for a single meal sold his inheritance (*that is, his birthright*) rights as the oldest son. Afterward, as you know, when he wanted to inherit this blessing, he was rejected. He could bring about no change of mind, though he sought the blessing with tears."

Verses 12 and 13 tell Christians not to be discouraged, for God is conscious of every trial they experience and will work things out to the good. As Christians go through the refining process, at times they may feel discouraged. But they need to keep their eyes focused on Christ, the Author and Finisher of their faith, who for the joy of seeing them in heaven endured hardships, even the hardship of the cross.

As Paul says in Romans 8:28, Christians know that all things work together for good to them who love God. Paul is not saying that everything comes directly from God. What he is proposing is that God allows everything—uses everything—for the believers' good because of His love for them and their love for Him.

Twofold Result

The result of this refining phenomenon is twofold. First, Christians become easier to live with because of God's unconditional love that dominates their behavior. Verse 14 brings this out. Paul says to make every effort to live in peace with all men and to be holy, for without holiness no one will see the Lord.

The word "holy" means set aside for God's use. Christians need to learn to walk daily in the Spirit rather than in the flesh. As they do this, the love of God will be shed abroad in their hearts. People will see Christ in them and the love He revealed while on earth.

The second thing that happens is that Christian lives begin to conform to the will of God rather than the will of the flesh. This is holy living.

Help to Believers

In verses 15-17 Paul says that such Christians bring tremendous help and encouragement to fellow believers as well as those who have backslidden. The church is a body, and when one part of the body suffers, the rest of the body must come to its aid. As Christians grow in maturity, they experience the life of Christ and can offer more and more help to fellow struggling believers. They learn to lift up rather than criticize those who struggle. They minister redemptively rather than judgmentally.

Echoes of the Old Covenant

Having pointed out the practical results of the New Covenant, Paul now turns his attention to what life was like under the Old Covenant. The Jewish readers of Hebrews were legalists before their conversion. They were under the heavy bondage of salvation by works. Now they have come under the New Covenant by the grace of the Lord, Jesus Christ and faith in Him. But there is danger that these early Christians will revert to Judaism, so Paul reminds them what life was like under the Old Covenant (Hebrews 12:18-21): "You have not come to a mountain that can be touched and that is burning with fire; to darkness, gloom and storm; to a trumpet blast or to such a voice speaking words that those who heard it begged that no further word be spoken to them, because they could not bear what was commanded. 'If even an animal touches the mountain, it must be stoned.' The sight was so terrifying that Moses said, 'I am trembling with fear.'"

The law as a means of salvation brings fear. Under grace, of course, the law becomes a delight, for it is no longer the means of salvation but keeping it becomes an outgrowth of Christian living.

This is the difference between the letter and the spirit of the law. Legalism is an outward conformity to the rules of the law—the do's and the don'ts—whereas in Christian living the spirit of the law is what counts—the spirit of love.

Love Fulfills the Law

Love is the fulfillment of the law, Paul says in Galatians 5:14 and Romans 13:8-10. This is the essence of the New Covenant—the writing of the law on the believers' hearts.

Paul is saying in these verses that to go back to the law as a means of salvation is to go back to living in gloom, darkness, and fear of the law's condemnation and death. In contrast to this life of fear, life under the New Covenant is peaceful, filled with joy and hope.

Even today many of God's people are still trapped in a subtle form of legalism and have no peace or joy, because they are constantly looking at their performance and seeing failure. Their self-esteem plummets and they grow discouraged. The devil then uses this situation as a stronghold from which to destroy their faith in Christ.

Jesus says, "Come to me, all you who are weary and burdened, and I will give you rest" (Matthew 11:28). Those who flocked to Jesus were primarily publicans and sinners, for they were the most discouraged members of society, under legalism. Legalism gave them no hope, but when Christ came on the scene, He told them that He had come to save not the righteous but sinners. So sinners flocked to Him to find peace and hope. This is what it means to live under the New Covenant.

Paul is essentially saying "Don't go back to Judaism with its gloom and darkness, fear and insecurity." He tells them in Hebrews 12:22 that in Christ, "you have come to Mount Zion."

Notice the contrast. In Hebrews 12:18 Paul talks about the mountain on fire—Mount Sinai. Under the law, God is a consuming fire but under grace, Mount Zion. Hence, "But you have come to Mount Zion to the heavenly Jerusalem, the city of the living God. You have come to thousands upon thousands of angels in joyful assembly."

What a wonderful exchange from legalism to salvation by grace, from Old Covenant to New Covenant! The New Covenant offers peace, hope, and joy.

A Contract Versus a Will

The Old Covenant is a contract between two parties—God and the Israelites, or Jews. In the Old Covenant God gives His law, a measuring stick of righteousness. In exchange the people say, "All that You say, we will do" (Exodus 19:8).

In other words the Jews of the Exodus want to see God eyeball to eyeball and say to Him, "You give us Your rules; we will keep them; You owe us salvation." They were sincere in what they asked for, but as we all know from Scripture, they could not keep that law. Not long after they agreed to keep the law, in fact, they made a calf out of gold and began worshipping it—something the law absolutely prohibited.

The New Covenant, on the other hand, is not a contract. It is a will—a promise. Like any will, it becomes effective only when the person who makes the will dies. When Christ died the promise of salvation God gave the Jewish nation and previously to the human race became a reality. Coming to Christ means coming to Mount Zion; the believer is coming to the heavenly Jerusalem, the city of the living God. The believer is coming before thousands upon thousands of angels in joyful assembly. This is what it means to be under the New Covenant. It is a life of peace, joy, and hope. For in Christ humanity is declared righteous, if by faith they accept the salvation offered.

God then looks at them as if they had never sinned. They stand complete in Christ (Colossians 2:10). They stand perfect. This is the difference between Abel's sacrifice, which was a type of the sacrifice (or will) of Christ, and Cain's sacrifice, which was salvation by works.

The Blood of Abel

In Hebrews 12:23 and 24 we continue reading: "To the church of the firstborn, whose names are written in heaven. You have come to God, the judge of all men, to the spirits of righteous men made perfect, to Jesus the mediator of a new covenant, and to the sprinkled blood that speaks a better word than the blood of Abel."

In the Old Testament, Adam's and Eve's adult children Cain and Abel offer sacrifices. The difference is that Abel's sacrifice is a confession of faith that one day his sin would be blotted out by the sacrifice of Christ, whereas Cain's sacrifice is one of works, "See what I produced. I am offering it to You, God, in exchange for salvation."

The Bible says Abel's sacrifice was accepted by God; Cain's was rejected. The Old Covenant can save no one. The Christian's hope is only in the New Covenant. There is no hope at Mount Sinai.

Mount Sinai is today a barren mountain, famous for its rocks and scorpions. Jerusalem, however, is set in a desert that through irrigation has been turned into a garden. These two locations express the differences between the law and grace.

The writer of Hebrews says, in Chapter 12, verses 25-27: "See to it that you do not refuse him who speaks. If they did not escape when they refused him who warned them on earth, how much less will we, if we turn away from him who warns us from heaven? At that time his voice shook the earth, but now he has promised, 'Once more I will shake not only the earth but also the heavens.'"

The words "once more" indicate the coming removal of that which can be shaken—that is, created things—so that what cannot be shaken may remain.

When God gave the law the mountain was covered with fire; it shook and the people were afraid. Paul is now saying that not only this world, but heaven itself will shake and anything that is not covered by the blood of Christ will be consumed by God, who is a consuming fire.

This is what verse 29 says, "Our God is a consuming fire." Everything that belongs to the world of sin will be consumed. The Christian's only hope is to seek shelter under the umbrella of Jesus Christ, for when a believer is in Christ, God no longer looks at him as a sinner but in His Son.

In Exodus, the Israelites paint blood on their doorposts so the Angel of Death will not strike the firstborn in the marked houses. When God sees the blood of Christ covering us, He no longer sees sinners but men and women who stand righteous in Christ—perfect before His law. But everything that is not of Christ will be consumed when Christ comes. Everything that belongs to sin will be destroyed and only that which has been cleansed of sin will remain.

No More Fire Protection

At the Second Coming of Christ, God will remove all barriers between Himself and sin. For now, God has built barriers between himself and sin so sinners can live without being consumed.

But at the Second Coming, Jesus will not come as a babe in a manger but as Lord, King of the universe. He will come in all His glory. And those who have turned away from the plan of salvation will become like firewood, consumed in the fire of His glory.

Because this is a matter of life and death, we will read two passages from the Old Testament about the glory of God. The first text is found in Exodus 24:17: "To the Israelites the glory of the Lord looked like a consuming fire on top of the mountain."

To the legalist the glory of the Lord looks like a consuming fire. The glory of God to the sinners who have rejected the gift of salvation becomes a consuming fire.

The second passage comes from Jeremiah 31:3, where God speaks to Israel in the context of the gospel and His love: "The Lord appeared to us in the past, saying, 'I have loved you with an everlasting love; I have drawn you with loving-kindness.'" The passage goes on to say it is because of this that humanity has not been consumed. But those who continue to reject Christ will be consumed by the brightness of His coming. Everything that is not of grace will be destroyed. This earth will be melting with fire, with the heat of the fire.

Salvation is a gift purchased at infinite cost to God. Christians must not treat this salvation lightly. They must not play games with it. To refuse the gift of salvation is to join the devil in the lake of fire. To accept Christ as Savior is to someday hear the words, "Come, you blessed of my Father inherit the kingdom prepared for you from the foundation of the world" (Matthew 25:34 [NKJV]).

Only those who have found safety in Christ will not be consumed by the fire and brightness of His Second Coming, for His blood has cleansed them from all sin.

Preparing for That Day

As we conclude this study of Hebrews 12, I plead with all Christian readers never to give up their faith in Christ, which has great recompense of reward. Do not turn your backs on the gift of salvation. I pray that your faith will endure unto the end in spite of the hardships of life.

When God allows Christians to pass through difficult times, He is refining their character, removing the rough edges, and taking away all that belongs to the flesh.

They count it as joy when they go through these times, for they recognize that God is refining them. As we read in Hebrews 12:11, when this refining work has done its job it produces the righteousness of Christ, which is their goal in the Christian walk.

Christians must keep their eyes focused on Christ, the Author and Finisher of their faith. Their faith needs to endure to the end. They are living at a time of this world's history when terrible things are happening around the world. Crime and immorality are on the rise and godliness is declining. Terrible things are coming.

As Paul told Timothy, those living in the last days will pass through major crises, some of which seem already upon us. Faith will be tested to the very limit.

Christians today must keep their eyes constantly focused on Christ. They must let nothing take away their faith and rob them of the joy and peace of salvation. They must keep their eyes focused on Him, the Author and Finisher of their salvation.

"You will be persecuted. You will be mistreated. You will be brought before synagogues, before governors and kings. Only those who endure unto the end will be saved," Jesus told his disciples.

God's great desire is to see as many as possible in heaven. But He respects the decisions of those who turn their backs on salvation. The blood of Christ can cleanse from all unrighteousness. But it can only be applied through faith of those who confess their sins and accept Jesus Christ as their Savior.

I pray that all who read these chapters will accept salvation by faith, grow to maturity in their Christian experiences, and endure to the end. Then one day we can all gather around the throne of Christ and sing "Hallelujah, Praise the Lord".

CHAPTER 20

Living the Christian Life
Hebrews 13:1-25

We now come to our final chapter in the book of Hebrews. During our past 19 studies I hope you have been blessed and that Christian readers, in particular, have been strengthened in their determination to remain faithful to Christ, come what may.

We now turn to the final chapter of Hebrews to study the 25 verses of Chapter 13.

Pauline Theology

As mentioned earlier in this book, the Greek used by the author of Hebrews is unlike the Greek used in any other epistle written by Paul. But though the language style is not Paul's, the theology most certainly is his.

I believe, therefore, that the writer of Hebrews is Paul, who apparently wrote the original version of this epistle in Aramaic rather than Greek. Someone else came along later—someone perhaps unacquainted with Paul's style in the Greek language—and translated the epistle for wider circulation.

Apart from this probability, we do know for certain that this book is inspired, and in this closing chapter, Paul gives wonderfully practical counsel on Christian living.

At the very heart of Paul's gospel is the truth he sets forth in Hebrews 10:38 and in other parts of the New Testament: "He that is just by faith shall live."

Salvation is by faith alone. He that is just, by faith shall live. Many Christians think the "living" begins after they go to heaven. But this is not biblical. To Paul, living the justified life begins the moment one becomes a Christian and receives the life of Christ through the new-birth experience.

The Gospel First

As with all Paul's epistles, he begins with the gospel but ends with applied Christian ethics, because for Paul the gospel is not just a theory. The gospel, as Paul tells us in his Epistle to the Romans, is the power of God unto salvation. It is the power of God not only to take us to heaven but to change lives now.

Jesus says in John 13:35 (NKJV): "By this shall all men know that you are my disciples when you have love one for another."

The word "love". He uses here is the unique New Testament term "agape,"an unconditional, selfless, unchangeable commitment manifested by God toward humankind. It is this love Christians must have for others.

Practical Counsel

Paul always ends his epistles with practical counsel on how to live the Christian life. And here in Hebrews they again find advice on how to live while they await Christ's return.

But before we can fully appreciate this counsel, we must consider an overarching test that must be applied when using the Bible as a practical guide in Christian living.

Principle and Practice

We must always make a distinction between a *principle* laid down in Scripture and a *practice*. While the *principles* of Christian living found in Scripture are eternal, the way Christians put those principles into practice can change from culture to culture, from era to era.

For example, Paul counsels Christian women in 1 Corinthians 11: 5 and 6 to cover their heads out of reverence to God when they go to church. In the same chapter he tells men not to wear their hair long.

Now, if we take this counsel and try to apply it in cultures far different from the Corinthian's of 2,000 years ago, we immediately face serious problems—for example, in cultures where women traditionally show reverence by *removing* head coverings and where *longer hair* for men is considered a norm of respectability.

Concerning every counsel given in Scripture, we have to ask

ourselves, "What is the fundamental principle behind this counsel and how should we apply this principle in modern practice?"

The *principles* found in Scripture are not only eternal but universal. The *practices* that emerge from these principles are governed by time and culture.

To illustrate, in the United States of America, especially in winter months, it is now perfectly acceptable for women to wear jeans or slacks. But when I was in Africa during the 1950s, for a Christian woman to wear slacks was forbidden, because back then only prostitutes wore jeans or slacks in that culture.

Naturally then, we advised American women coming to Africa as missionaries to kindly leave their jeans and slacks back home. What was becoming perfectly acceptable for respectable women in America was still absolutely unacceptable in Africa.

The principle that Christian women should dress and behave with Christian modesty remained absolutely the same on both continents. The only difference was in how the principle was applied.

Two Great Principles

In reviewing all the guidelines for Christian living in Scripture, we discover two overarching principles. These two principles are found together in 1 Corinthians 10:31 and 32, where Paul says, "So whether you eat or drink or whatever you do, do it all for the glory of God. Do not cause anyone to stumble, whether Jews, Greeks or the church of God."

Verse 31 cautions us to do nothing that would get in the way of our relationship with God; Verse 32 speaks of our responsibility as role models to others, both inside and outside the church.

To apply these principles, we turn first to a New Testament example. There is a question—an issue— about whether Christians should eat food offered to idols. Christians, of course, *never* pray or sacrifice to idols, but pagans do and regularly bring food to offer to various deities.

The priests of these pagan gods accept this food and in turn sell it in the marketplace as a source of income. Because the priests pay nothing for the food, they can afford to undersell conventional food merchants. And since the customs of the day call for food offered to idols to be of top quality, this food is not only cheaper, it is often better.

Many less-affluent Christians buy this food, not out of love for the idols, but because it's a smart way to stretch the food dollar.

Other Christians of very sensitive conscience, however, feel that no Christian should *ever* buy or eat such food. The discussion grows so heated it produces a split in the early Christian church. But Paul refuses to take sides, saying only, "Let each one be persuaded in his own mind because everyone who lives, lives unto the Lord."

In other words, the first principle of Christian living is that followers of Christ should do nothing that mars their relationship with God. If eating food offered to idols interferes with that relationship, by all means stop eating it! But if not, feel free to buy and eat.

The second overarching principle is that Christians should do nothing to interfere with another person's spiritual direction and development in Christ. If eating certain kinds of foods will cause somebody's faith to falter, Paul says, "Do not touch it, not for your sake but for his sake."

Paul then adds in verse 33: "Even as I try to please everybody in every way. For I am not seeking my own good but the good of many, so that they may be saved."

These are the two big ethical principles of everyday Christian life, and with these in mind, let us consider Paul's counsel on Christian ethics found in Hebrews 13.

Ethics in Hebrews 13

The counsel itself can be divided into two parts: verses 1-6 identify how Christians should live in the world. Verses 7-25 deal primarily with Christian behavior in the church.

First let us read the opening six verses before studying them in detail: "Keep on loving each other as brothers. Do not forget to entertain strangers, for by so doing some people have entertained angels without knowing it. Remember those in prison as if you were their fellow prisoners, and those who are mistreated as if you yourselves were suffering. Marriage should be honored by all, and the marriage bed kept pure, for God will judge the adulterer and all the sexually immoral. Keep your lives free from the love of money and be content with what you have, because God has said, 'Never will I leave you; never will I forsake you.' So we say with confidence, 'The Lord is my helper; I will not be afraid. What can man do to me?'"

The counsel to treat others as Christians would like to be treated themselves is based on the Second Great Commandment—that believers should love their neighbors as themselves. Two other passages bring this out, one spoken by Jesus Christ and the other by the apostle Paul.

In Matthew 22, a Jewish lawyer—one with profound knowledge of the books of Moses—approaches Jesus to test Him, at the urging of a group of Pharisees (verses 34 and 35).

Verses 35 and 36 say: "One of them, an expert in the law, tested him with this question: 'Teacher, which is the greatest commandment in the law?'"

The question seems simple and straightforward. Jesus' reply is likewise direct and unequivocal: "Love the Lord your God with all your heart and with all your soul and with all your mind. This is the first and greatest commandment."

Jesus is quoting from Deuteronomy 6:5. He then refers to a passage in Leviticus 19:18, saying: "And the second is like it. Love your neighbor as yourself."

The lawyer asks Jesus, "What is the greatest commandment in the books of Moses?" Jesus quotes two texts from the writings of Moses, the book of the law, to point out love lies at the very heart of the law—it is the very spirit of the law.

Then Jesus adds in Matthew 22:40, "All the law and the Prophets hang on these two commandments."

When we look at the Ten Commandments (the Decalogue), we discover that the first four commandments have to do with a Christian's relationship with God and the last six deal with a Christian's relationship with fellow men.

But let us not become confused. Jesus says, "Love your neighbor as yourself," He does not say, "Try to love your neighbor as yourself." Human love is egocentric. We love ourselves unconditionally and spontaneously. We love ourselves when we are good and when we are bad. When we are given a traffic ticket for speeding, we plead for mercy from the policeman, not because we love the law of the land or the policeman, but because we love our pockets. Human love is unconditional toward one's own self. Christ is saying in Matthew

22 that we should love our neighbor in the same way—that is, unconditionally, the way we love ourselves.

Once again, the first commandment is to love God with all one's heart, with all one's mind, and with all one's soul. The second commandment is to love one's neighbor as one loves his- or herself.

Love is indeed the fulfillment of all the law, as brought out in Romans 13:8-10, where again Paul gives counsel on Christian ethics. In Romans 12-15, Paul talks about living the Christian life, for the just begin living differently from the moment they accept Christ.

"Let no debt remain outstanding, except the continuing debt to love one another, for he who loves his fellowman has fulfilled the law,"Paul says. He then quotes the last six commandments of the Decalogue and ends up with verse 10: "Love does no harm to its neighbor, therefore love is the fulfillment of the law."

Hebrews 13:1-3 encapsulates the two great commandments, especially the last six spelled out in practical language. We need to treat our fellow human beings as we would treat ourselves.

In Hebrews 13:4 Paul says, "Avoid immoral life and the practices of illicit sex." As Paul advised the Christians in Rome, we must not fit into this world's mould. Today's world offers almost complete sexual freedom. Thousands of couples are living together outside of marriage, and Paul says here that Christians must avoid the practice, and even the appearance, of evil.

In Hebrews 13:5 and 6, Paul addresses the issue of being content with what God has provided. Love of money—not money itself—is where danger lies. One way the devil tries to pull believers out of Christ is to dangle the world's trinkets in front of them.

Learning To Be Content

Paul's counsel in Hebrews 13 is for Christians to learn to be content, whatever circumstances may be. When he writes to young Timothy, Paul gives much the same sound advice and warning in 1 Timothy 6:6-10: "But godliness with contentment is great gain. For we brought nothing into the world, and we can take nothing out of it. But if we have food and clothing, we will be content with that. People who want to get rich fall into temptation and a trap and into many foolish and harmful desires that plunge men into ruin and destruction. For the love of money is a root of all kinds of evil. Some people, eager for money, have wandered from the faith and pierced themselves with many griefs."

It is not wrong to have money. It is not wrong to be rich. But Christians must not make materialism a god, because the devil will use this to persuade them to turn their backs on Christ. As we have been studying throughout Hebrews, when Christians turn their backs on Christ, they give up their hope of salvation.

These first seven verses of Hebrews 13 deal with Christian behavior, Christian living, and Christian relationships. This counsel about living the Christian life in this world while awaiting the Lord's return is based on the fundamental truth that Christians are not of the world.

"Love not the world, nor the things of the world, "John says. Then he defines the world as "the lust of the flesh, the lust of the eyes and the pride of life." (See 1 John 2:15.16) These belong to the world but not to God.

General Advice

Turning to Hebrews 13:8-25, Paul gives advice to Jewish believers of his day on how they should live in the church. The first seven verses deal with how Christians should live in the world and what their relationship should be with their fellow men. But now he examines relationships between fellow Christians.

Hebrews 13:8-15 begins: "Remember your leaders, who spoke the word of God to you. Consider the outcome of their way of life and imitate their faith. Jesus Christ is the same yesterday and today and forever. Do not be carried away by all kinds of strange teachings. It is good for our hearts to be strengthened by grace, not by ceremonial foods, which are of no value to those who eat them."

In other words, Paul is asking the believers not to be trapped again by legalism in all its forms. "We have an altar from which those who minister at the tabernacle have no right to eat,"he continues. "The high priest carries the blood of animals into the Most Holy Place as a sin offering, but the bodies are burned outside the camp. And so Jesus also suffered outside the city gate to make the people holy through his own blood. Let us, then, go to him outside the camp, bearing the disgrace he bore. For here we do not have an enduring city, but we are looking for the city that is to come. Through Jesus, therefore, let us continually offer to God a sacrifice of praise— the fruit of lips that confess his name. And do not forget to do good and to share with others, for with such sacrifices God is pleased.

"Obey your leaders and submit to their authority. They keep watch over you as men who must give an account. Obey them so that their work will be a joy, not a burden, for that would be of no advantage to you. Pray for us. We are sure that we have a clear conscience and desire to live honorably in every way. I particularly urge you to pray so that I may be restored to you soon. May the God of peace, who through the blood of the eternal covenant brought back from the dead our Lord Jesus, that great Shepherd of the sheep, equip you with everything good for doing his will, and may he work in us what is pleasing to him through Jesus Christ, to whom be glory for ever and ever. Brothers, I urge you to bear with my word of exhortation, for I have written you only a short letter. I want you to know that our brother Timothy has been released. If he arrives soon, I will come with him to see you. Greet all your leaders and all God's people. Those from Italy send you their greetings. Grace be with you all."

Four Short Lessons

We can briefly divide this counsel into four parts:
(1)   Learn to live as the saints of old, whose eyes were focused on Christ;
(2)   Beware of false teachers with false teachings that pervert the gospel;
(3)   When mistreated, be willing to suffer and avoid retaliation, even as Christ did, and finally,
(4)   Be good citizens. Witness the love of Christ. Pray for each other and let the blessed hope fill your heart with joy and peace.

To these words, I add, "Amen". May God take this truth, establish you in Christ and produce fruits in your life. And one day may we meet in the kingdom of God through Jesus Christ.